25 Ready-to-Use
Sustainable Living Programs for Libraries

25
READY-TO-USE
Sustainable Living
Programs
for Libraries

EDITED BY **ELLYSSA KROSKI**

ALA
Editions

CHICAGO | 2023

ELLYSSA KROSKI is the director of information technology and marketing at the New York Law Institute, as well as an award-winning editor and author of 75 books. She is a librarian, an adjunct faculty member at San Jose State University, and an international conference speaker. She can be found at www.amazon.com/author/ellyssa.

© 2023 by the American Library Association

Extensive effort has gone into ensuring the reliability of the information in this book; however, the publisher makes no warranty, express or implied, with respect to the material contained herein.

ISBN: 978-0-8389-3649-8 (paper)

Library of Congress Cataloging-in-Publication Data
Names: Kroski, Ellyssa, editor.
Title: 25 ready-to-use sustainable living programs for libraries / Ellyssa Kroski.
Other titles: Twenty-five ready-to-use sustainable living programs for libraries
Description: Chicago : ALA Editions, 2023. | Includes bibliographical references and index. | Summary: "25 Ready-to-Use Sustainable Living Programs for Libraries is an all-in-one guide to how to plan, organize, and run sustainable living programs in libraries"—Provided by publisher.
Identifiers: LCCN 2022032690 | ISBN 9780838936498 (paperback)
Subjects: LCSH: Libraries—Activity programs—United States. | Sustainable living—Study and teaching—Activity programs.
Classification: LCC Z716.33 .A13 2022 | DDC 025.5—dc23/eng/20220713
LC record available at https://lccn.loc.gov/2022032690

Book design by Alejandra Diaz in the Utopia Std and Bilo typefaces.

♾ This paper meets the requirements of ANSI/NISO Z39.48-1992 (Permanence of Paper).

Printed in the United States of America
27 26 25 24 23   5 4 3 2 1

CONTENTS

PART I: GARDENING PROGRAMS

PART II: PRESERVATION PROGRAMS

PART III: PIONEER CRAFTS PROGRAMS

PREFACE

In the wake of the COVID-19 pandemic, interest levels in sustainability and self-reliance topics have risen considerably among library patrons of all ages. Libraries of all types are enhancing their programming by embracing these timely topics and providing much sought-after instruction. They are organizing instructional workshops, forming gardening clubs, creating community gardens, building beekeeping exhibits, teaching patrons about reducing waste and sustainable food sources, and more.

25 Ready-to-Use Sustainable Living Programs for Libraries is an all-in-one guide to how to plan, organize, and run sustainable living programs in libraries. Programs range from gardening and herbal medicine to teaching pioneer crafts, homesteading topics such as composting and beekeeping, and hosting food preservation events.

Each program walks the reader through step-by-step instructions for how to prepare for and host these events, including a materials and equipment list, a budget, and recommendations for age ranges and type of library. Programs range in cost, topic, and difficulty, so there is something for every size and type of library, both rural and urban. The authors of these programs are knowledgeable experts and professionals from the library field who are offering real-world programming ideas for public, school, and academic libraries.

ACKNOWLEDGMENTS

I would like to heartily thank all the knowledgeable librarians and specialists who shared their time, experience, and expertise in this book. It was a pleasure to work with all of you.

INTRODUCTION
Building a Sustainable and Self-Reliant Lifestyle

ELLYSSA KROSKI

Sustainable living involves making changes in your everyday life to ensure that you leave the planet a better place after you're gone. These changes can include reducing waste, recycling, saying no to plastic, growing your own food, repairing rather than replacing, and reducing your overall carbon footprint. This doesn't have to happen overnight; it can start with baby steps such as adopting reusable shopping bags, buying from local farmers, and carpooling.

Living in a time of a worldwide pandemic, supply chain shortages, civil unrest, and the ongoing global political uncertainty of today's world has awakened an increased interest in sustainable and self-reliant living. In what *Forbes* magazine has dubbed an "urban exodus," many Americans have chosen to leave densely populated cities behind in favor of rural locales where they can build a more self-sufficient lifestyle.[1]

Far from the need to social distance or battle morning traffic, I walk out to my chicken coop each day at sunrise to collect a basket full of pastel-colored eggs from my Easter Egger chickens that lay pink, blue, and olive-green eggs and that serenade me with the egg song which they sing in order to congratulate themselves after a fresh one is laid. I am one of the many people who have opted for the freedom of building a self-sufficient and sustainable way of life during the COVID-19 pandemic.

I traded my four-bedroom, 2,500-square-foot home in a planned community for 14 acres in the country and a 1,100-square-foot manufactured home with just enough room for everything I need, at a fraction of the mortgage and energy consumption. I work from home, managing technology and marketing projects for my library, and I wander outside when I need a break, and pet my goats and sheep and tinker around with my gardens and hothouses. With no daily commute, I save a ton in gas as well as my own precious time while also helping to reduce my carbon footprint.

Rather than turn on the television every night, I'll often start a fire with firewood cut from my land and look up at a sky filled with stars unlike

FIGURE 0.1 | The author bottle-feeding a lamb on her homestead

anything I'd ever laid eyes on living in the city. I take pride in my gardens and the ability to grow not just my own vegetables, but fodder plants to feed some of my animals, the herbs and spices that I love to cook with daily such as basil, oregano, sage, parsley, dill, cilantro, rosemary, and chives, and my own loofah sponges. And I have fruit cages protecting my blackberry, raspberry, and blueberry bushes alongside the lemon, lime, and banana trees that I hope to harvest fruit from this year.

In the short time that I've lived here, I have learned to can, freeze, and dehydrate my vegetables, beef, herbs, and flowers; cook and bake on a daily basis; cut and style my own hair; and make my own beauty products. After living in New York City's Upper East Side for over twenty-five years (and stopping for a slice each night on the way home from work) and then in the major tourist destination of Myrtle Beach, South Carolina, this is quite a change, but I couldn't be happier.

My family has since followed me on this adventure, with my sister and parents each adding their own homes to the property to create a family homestead we call "The Shire" where we share resources, experience, and expertise. This past winter, a cooperative purchase of a half a beef steer from a local cattle farmer amounted to a fraction of the cost of purchasing meat at the grocery store, saved us all countless trips to said store, and fed all three households on the homestead well into the spring. On holidays we have but to roam across the meadow to gather, and if one of us needs help with a project or simply runs out of sugar, the family is only steps away.

FIGURE 0.2 | The author's
goat and sheep meadow

This has been a huge learning curve for me because I've never met anyone who has done anything like this, and I would have loved guidance on any number of topics from my local library. Libraries in both urban and rural areas are in a unique position to be able to offer library patrons timely instructional programs that teach this type of sustainable and self-reliant living. From homesteading topics such as how to reduce food waste to creating DIY cleaning products, to growing and preserving one's own food, libraries can support patrons who wish to live "off the grid," those who want to start their own hobby farm, others who are seeking to create a homestead, or patrons who simply want to learn how to garden.

This book was compiled to help guide librarians who want to institute these types of programs in their libraries.

READING LIST

The following is my personal bookshelf of homesteading, gardening, preserving, and hobby farm books and magazines that I own and recommend. Each of these works helped to give me a great start on this rewarding adventure.

Books

Gardening

Akeroyd, S. 2011. *The Complete Gardener's Guide: Everything You Need to Know to Create and Care for Your Garden*. New York: DK Publishing.

Ashworth, S. 1991. *Seed to Seed*. Decorah, IA: Seed Savers Publications.

Chevallier, A. 2016. *Encyclopedia of Herbal Medicine: 550 Herbs and Remedies for Common Ailments*. 3rd edition. New York: DK Publishing.

Chevallier, A. 2018. *Herbal Remedies Handbook: More Than 140 Plant Profiles; Remedies for over 50 Common Conditions*. New York: DK Publishing.

Foret, R. 2017. *Alchemy of Herbs: Transform Everyday Ingredients into Foods & Remedies That Heal*. Carlsbad, CA: Hay House.

Gutierrez, A. G., and M. Gray. 2017. *Potted: Make Your Own Stylish Garden Containers*. Portland, OR: Timber Press.

Holmes, R., and R. Buchanan. 2010. *Southeast Home Landscaping*, 3rd edition. La Vergne, TN: Fox Chapel Publishing.

Jabbour, N. 2018. *Niki Jabbour's Veggie Garden Remix: 224 New Plants to Shake Up Your Garden and Add Variety, Flavor, and Fun*. North Adams, MA: Storey Publishing.

Karsten, J. 2019. *Straw Bale Gardens Complete: Breakthrough Method for Growing Vegetables Anywhere, Earlier and with No Weeding*. Beverly, MA: Cool Springs Press.

Shaffer, M. 2001. *Planning & Planting a Moon Garden*. North Adams, MA: Storey Publishing.

Preservation

America's Test Kitchen. 2016. *Foolproof Preserving: A Guide to Small Batch Jams, Jellies, Pickles, Condiments, and More*. Brookline, MA: America's Test Kitchen.

Cancler, C. 2020. *Complete Dehydrator Cookbook: How to Dehydrate Fruit, Vegetables, Meat & More*. Emeryville, CA: Rockridge Press.

Kingry, J., and L. Devine. 2020. *Ball Complete Book of Home Preserving: 400 Delicious and Creative Recipes for Today*. Toronto, ON: Robert Rose.

Marrone, T. 2018. *The Beginner's Guide to Dehydrating Food: How to Preserve All Your Favorite Vegetables, Fruits, Meats, and Herbs*. North Adams, MA: Storey Publishing.

Hobby Farms

Bennett, B. 2018. *Storey's Guide to Raising Rabbits: Breeds, Care, Housing.* North Adams, MA: Storey Publishing.

Bradshaw, A. 2020. *The Beginner's Guide to Raising Goats: How to Keep a Happy Herd.* Emeryville, CA: Rockridge Press.

Damerow, G., and Overdrive Inc. 2011. *The Backyard Homestead Guide to Raising Farm Animals.* North Adams, MA: Storey Publishing.

Ekarius, C. 2011. *How to Build Animal Housing: 60 Plans for Coops, Hutches, Barns, Sheds, Pens, Nestboxes, Feeders, Stanchions, and Much More.* North Adams, MA: Storey Publishing.

Garman, J. 2020. *50 Do-It-Yourself Projects for Keeping Goats.* New York: Skyhorse Publishing.

Hyman, F. 2018. *Hentopia: Create a Hassle-Free Habitat for Happy Chickens: 21 Innovative Projects.* North Adams, MA: Storey Publishing.

Kuo, A., and B. Alexander. 2021. *The Beginner's Guide to Raising Chickens: How to Raise a Happy Backyard Flock.* Emeryville, CA: Rockridge Press.

Simmons, P. 2019. *Storey's Guide to Raising Sheep: Breeding, Care, Facilities.* 5th edition. North Adams, MA: Storey Publishing.

Weaver, S., A. L. Hansen, C., Langlois, A. B. McFarlen, and C. McLaughlin, 2015. *Hobby Farm Animals.* Irvine, CA: i-5 Publishing.

Homesteading

Carlsen, S., Philip Schmidt, Sarah Guare, Carleen Madigan, Elayne Sears, Bruce Kieffer, and Tom Thulen. 2014. *The Backyard Homestead Book of Building Projects.* North Adams, MA: Storey Publishing.

Gehring, A. R. 2011. *The Homesteading Handbook: A Back to Basics Guide to Growing Your Own Food, Canning, Keeping Chickens, Generating Your Own Energy, Crafting, Herbal Medicine, and More.* New York: Skyhorse Publishing.

Hansen, A. L. 2017. *The Backyard Homestead Seasonal Planner: What to Do & When to Do It.* North Adams, MA: Storey Publishing.

Madigan, C. 2009. *The Backyard Homestead: Produce All the Food You Need on Just a Quarter-Acre!* North Adams, MA: Storey Publishing.

Markham, B. L. 2011. *Mini Farming: Self-Sufficiency on ¼ Acre.* London: Right Way.

Seymour, J., and W. Sutherland. 2018. *The Self-Sufficient Life and How to Live It.* New York: DK Publishing.

Strawbridge, D., and J. Strawbridge. 2020. *Self-Sufficiency for the 21st Century: The Complete Guide to Sustainable Living Today.* New York: DK Publishing.

Magazines

Chickens, a bimonthly magazine from the editors of *Hobby Farms*: www.hobby farms.com/subscribe-new/

Hobby Farms, a bimonthly magazine: www.hobbyfarms.com/subscribe-new/

Mother Earth News, a bimonthly magazine: https://store.motherearthnews.com /magazine/mother-earth-news

The New Pioneer, a quarterly magazine: www.amazon.com/Harris-Publications -New-Pioneer/dp/B00F8P2VOK

Self-Reliance, a quarterly magazine: www.backwoodshome.com/shop/product/ sr-one-or-two-years-subscription/

Special Issues

Chickens Magazine, "Chicken Coops & Playgrounds Special Issue": www.hobby farms.com/back-issues/

Chickens Magazine, "Ducks 101 Special Issue: The Essential Guide to Raising Waterfowl, Everything You Need to Know, and More": www.hobbyfarms .com/back-issues/

Hobby Farms, "Goats 101 Special Issue: The Essential Guide to Raising Goats," www.hobbyfarms.com/product/goats-101/

Mother Earth News, "Beginner's Guide to Living on Less," https://store.mother earthnews.com/product/mother-earth-news-beginner-s-guide-to-living -on-less

Outdoor Life, "Live Off the Grid: Get There – Survive There – Thrive There," www.amazon.com/Outdoor-Life-Live-Off-Grid/dp/168330974X

NOTE

1. Chris Dorsey, "Pandemic Leads to Urban Exodus as Families Turn to Self-Reliance and Off-the-Grid Living," *Forbes*, June 10, 2020, www.forbes .com/sites/chrisdorsey/2020/06/10/pandemic-leads-to-urban-exodus-as -families-turn-to-self-reliance-and-off-the-grid-living/?sh=4cabac10cdaa.

PART I
Gardening Programs

Coordinating Gardening and Sustainability Programs with Local Experts

ANNA FRANTZ

The interest in all subjects related to gardening and sustainability continues to grow in library communities, especially for those who are trying to be more environmentally conscious. As librarians, we want to support our communities' interests and ensure access to these kinds of programs. However, if one has limited experience with this subject, planning these programs can feel overwhelming. Fortunately, most communities, whether large or small, have gardening and sustainability experts who are happy to share their knowledge. This chapter will provide examples of organizations your library can contact to host programs, as well as the key details you'll want to discuss with them to ensure a successful program.

Age Range	Library Type	Cost Estimate
Kids (ages 3–7) Tweens (ages 8–12) Young adults (ages 13–18) Adults	Public libraries	$0–$200

3

Cost Considerations

The costs for featuring presenters can vary. Most government organizations and nonprofits will present for free because education and outreach are part of their mission; in return, you can have your library promote their organization and purchase any supplies the presenters may need for their programs. If your budget is limited, check with your local plant nurseries to see if they are willing to donate materials in exchange for advertising their business. Some presenters may have all the supplies they already need, or they may only be showing a PowerPoint. If presenters have published books on the subject they're speaking about, allow them to sell their books after the program.

OVERVIEW

Regardless of the topic, you should schedule each program for at least an hour and a half; if the program requires participants to create a project or gets hands-on, or you would like time for a Q&A following the presentation, schedule it for two hours. Have one staff person, typically the coordinator, stay with the presenter during the program in case they need any assistance, such as with technology or handing out materials. The attendance cap for each program will vary depending on the size of your room as well as what kind of program it is; for example, lectures can encompass more people, whereas workshops can vary in size, depending on your budget for supplies or whether presenters need to be more hands-on with instruction.

NECESSARY EQUIPMENT AND MATERIALS

Each program will require different materials to run successfully. However, most will require:

- A laptop with at least two HDMI ports to allow connection with a projector and a USB
- A projector screen
- A stand to hold the laptop and projector
- A table if the presenter wants to display any visual materials that correspond with their program, such as any garden-related equipment, handouts, or books they have for sale

Examples of Organizations to Contact

The following list of potential presenters is a small sample, but it is a good start for those beginning to plan programs with outside experts. Some of the programs suggested may only be offered seasonally. Additionally, depending on the size of your city, you may not have access to some of these resources.

To contact presenters, simply conduct an internet search containing your city, state, and the subject or organization you would like to feature a program about. Searches can be subject-specific (e.g., "Albuquerque, NM aeroponics") or organization-based (e.g., "Salt Lake City, UT Master Gardeners"). Many cities have various nonprofit or government organizations that specialize in these subjects but which may not be listed on national websites or registries. In addition to searching online, attending city, state, and county fairs can provide great networking opportunities and is one of the best ways to learn what the local organizations are and what educational outreach they conduct.

- *Beekeepers:* Programs include beekeeping basics and plants that encourage pollinators, including your native bees. Certified beekeepers, both private and commercial, can be found through state associations, county extension programs, your city's Parks and Recreation Department, as well as garden centers.
- *County extension programs:* Programs are extensive and diverse and can include canning, community gardening, and aeroponics and hydroponics. 4-H Youth Development, Master Gardeners, and Master Composters are all examples of county extension programs.
- *Garden centers:* A garden center is a retail operation that sells plants and related products and supplies for domestic gardening. Each garden center is unique, and many have members clubs, which offer price discounts in exchange for a membership fee. Check and see which member clubs your local garden center is involved with regarding the topics of self-sufficiency and sustainability. Their programs will be similar to those of Master Gardener organizations and county extension programs.
- *Master Gardener organizations:* Master Gardeners are a great resource, as each organization typically has multiple volunteers who are trained in a variety of areas and can offer more specific, advanced programs in addition to introductory 101s. Programs are diverse and far-reaching

and can include raised-bed gardening, saving seeds, and growing trees, to name just a few topics. Check to see if your local Master Gardener's organization has a speakers bureau. If they do, contacting their liaison is the best way to get acquainted with the members who teach on the subjects you're most interested in.

- *Master Composters:* Programs include vermicomposting (composting with worms), Bokashi composting (fermented composting), and area-specific composting (e.g., desert composting). Check your local county extension to see if your locality has a Master Composter. If not, most Master Gardeners will offer basic composting programs.
- *Herbalists:* Programs include herbal medicine, edible plants, and aromatherapy.
- *Parks and Recreation Department:* Programs may include how to build a community garden and backyard orchard culture (i.e., how to grow, care for, and prune home orchard trees, fruiting vines, canes, and other fruiting perennials). Check and see if your local Parks and Recreation Department has an open space or a botanical garden. Programs vary depending on your location, as they focus on local plants and natural resources.
- *City water authorities and utility departments:* Programs may include drip irrigation and rainwater harvesting.

STEP-BY-STEP INSTRUCTIONS

Once you decide what kind of program you want to host and with whom, contact the organization and propose that your library would like to partner with them to host an educational program. Do this at least three months before you'd like to host the program. E-mail is usually the best way to do this, so you'll have in writing what you have already discussed with the organization. Be specific about what kind of program you want to have. If you're contacting a general organization such as Master Gardeners, they'll need to know what you want featured in order to connect you with the person best suited to lead the program.

After making initial introductions, the key things to discuss are the date and time of the event, the event's title and summary, whether registration is required, and the program's budget (materials fees as well as a possible speaker fee). In the program's summary, make sure to include the presenter's name, the organization they work for, and their qualifications. For online advertisements, make sure to link the organization's website with your program summary.

At least one month before the event, design a promotional flyer that can be used in your library's building as well as online, including social media. E-mail a PDF of the flyer to the presenter so they can approve it and use it to promote their program on their organization's website and social media. If you don't have to follow a certain format for your library's promotional materials, it is worth asking if the presenter has a flyer already created for past programs they've hosted. Although this advertising method can save a lot of time for you and your presenter, make sure that all critical information is changed on the flyer if you do this, such as the date and time, location, and registration procedures.

A couple of weeks before the program, make sure you have all the materials your presenter will need. If the amount of materials is dependent upon registration, you may have to wait until registration for the event closes, which could range from a week to just a few days before the program. If the program requires technology, such as a PowerPoint, ensure that everything works a couple of days ahead of time, and have the presenter save the PowerPoint onto a USB in case there are any issues with the internet connection. The presenter should come at least thirty minutes before the program begins in order to make sure that the space, technology, and materials are set up correctly.

RECOMMENDED NEXT PROJECTS

The great thing about coordinating with outside organizations is that you can plan many gardening and sustainability programs without having to come up with all the instructions and materials yourself. If your initial program goes well, see about hosting a program once a month. If your staff and budget allow, you can also look at hosting a series during peak gardening or sustainability months (e.g., planning for your spring garden or weekly programs in April for National Gardening Month).

Growing Vegetables Outside in Winter

NANCY GRIFFITHS

I n this program, participants will learn how to set up a vegetable bed for growing vegetables in the wintertime. They will also learn how to grow seedlings to transplant into that bed in the late summer or early fall. If your library has space for an outdoor demonstration bed, then you can grow vegetables there along with your participants. You can also guide participants in setting up their winter garden beds at home through a simple instructional program. And optionally, you can grow seedlings on a display table in the library, and then give them away to those who attend your program, in order to both give them a head-start on transplanting and to show them how the seedlings can be started indoors, even without having an outdoor demonstration garden bed at the library.

One of the perks of winter gardening in low tunnels is the absence of insects and diseases! Some vegetables can be harvested throughout the winter and some will be ready to harvest in the early spring. This chapter will cover helping patrons grow seedlings indoors in the late summer or early autumn using a heat mat and grow lights, and setting up a frame outdoors to protect the vegetables over the winter using wire garden hoops and frost cloths. You will also learn how to teach patrons to amend the soil in their vegetable beds prior to transplanting their vegetable seedlings and how to provide water for their plants over the winter.

Age Range	Library Type	Cost Estimate
Adults (children can also participate if supervised)	Public libraries	$0–$250 minimum, but can cost more, depending on how elaborate your participants would like the program to be.

Cost Considerations

To grow seedlings, a minimum purchase of organic seeds, organic potting soil, organic seedling fertilizer, one heat mat, a tray for seedlings, and one grow light (with or without a stand) is highly recommended. If the grow light is purchased without a stand, then you or your participants will need to have an alternative way to be able to hang the grow light over the seedlings at home.

To set up the vegetable bed for winter, a minimum purchase of organic fertilizer and/or compost, frost cloth, and wire garden hoops is recommended. Materials other than wire hoops can be used to create a tunnel for the frost cloth, such as PVC piping, wood, and so on. However, wire hoops are the least expensive type, and the costs will increase when stronger, sturdier materials are chosen.

OVERVIEW

One person can lead this program. The time frame for this program is about an hour and a half to two hours. There are three choices:

1. You can create an instructional PowerPoint (this option requires only the PowerPoint, laptop, and projector—nothing else).
2. You can grow seedlings to give away during the program, use the materials as a teaching tool for how to grow the seedlings, and add a PowerPoint with instructions on how to set up the vegetable bed for winter.

3. You can grow seedlings as in step 2 and also create a vegetable bed for winter with the program participants in your demonstration garden bed.

NECESSARY EQUIPMENT AND MATERIALS

Materials for Growing Seedlings

- Organic, non-GMO (i.e., non-genetically modified) vegetable seeds for "greens" (e.g., chard, lettuce, kale, etc.)
- Organic potting soil or seedling mix
- Organic fertilizer for seedlings or organic liquid seaweed fertilizer
- Plastic containers for growing seedlings (e.g., yogurt cups, tofu containers, etc.)
- Something to poke holes in the bottoms of the plastic containers (e.g., knife, awl, etc.)
- Larger plastic containers (e.g., salad container) to create a "greenhouse"
- A heat mat
- A tray to hold the seedlings under the lights (this will be used for bottom watering)
- One grow light with stand
- Or one grow light without a stand, but with chains or strong string for hanging the light above the seedlings

FIGURE 2.1 | An example of a grow light without a stand

Materials for Setting up the Vegetable Bed

- Organic fertilizer amendments and/or compost
- Frost cloth (It is not recommended to use row covers, plastic, sheets, or cloth materials because a floating row cover is a light material primarily meant to protect vegetables from insects and birds. It can be used to shield vegetables from a light frost at the end of the season, but it will not guard against freezing temperatures. For a brief overnight freeze, you can cover vegetables with a light sheet or blanket [be sure they won't break the stems of your plants] and for added protection, you can cover the cloth with plastic, but covering vegetables with plastic alone will damage your plants. Sheets or other fabrics are not designed to allow the proper amount of light through the material to grow plants, they do not hold the heat inside the structure, and they cannot be used long-term over a winter to protect from freezing temperatures.)
- Wire garden hoops (rope and stakes might be required if you choose wire hoops that have "eyes"—where the wire creates a loop for rope to be threaded through)
- Rocks, bricks, and/or boards for holding down the frost cloth at its edges

Recommended but Optional Materials

If you (or your participants) choose not to grow your own seedlings, they will need to be purchased so they can be transplanted to the vegetable bed in the late summer or early fall. This should be done at least one month before the first frost in your area (enough time for the transplants to take root and begin growing).

STEP-BY-STEP INSTRUCTIONS

Preparation: Growing Seedlings

Start the seedlings at least one month before your program on a display table advertising the program. For drainage, punch holes in the bottoms of the small containers you will use to grow the seedlings. Label each container with the variety of seed you're growing in it (e.g., rainbow chard). Lightly fill the containers with pre-moistened organic seedling mix or a light potting soil, but don't pack down the soil in the containers. Pre-moisten the soil by adding some water to it in a separate bucket and then mix until the soil is moist but not soaked. Place the containers inside a larger plastic container, put a touch of water in the bottom of the larger container, put the lid on, and place it on top of the heat mat. A heat mat is used to warm the soil in the container for faster seed germination. This will create a "greenhouse" for the seeds to germinate. You won't need to open the larger container until the seeds germinate (small sprouts will appear).

Not all containers inside your small greenhouse will germinate at the same time. When one germinates, take its container out and replace the lid on the greenhouse. If the greenhouse is looking dry, add a touch of water to the bottom of it before closing the lid.

Place the germinated seedlings on a tray under the grow light. Keep the light no higher than 2 inches above the seedlings, otherwise the seedlings might become "leggy" trying to reach for the light. In order to bottom-water your seedlings, you should fill this tray with water for twenty minutes every other day, and then drain the water. Do not water the soil from the top. Once the "true" leaves appear, add a few drops of organic liquid seaweed fertilizer to the water each time you water your seedlings. (The first leaves to appear are the cotyledons; true leaves then follow.)

When your seedlings are ready to transplant (minimum 4–5 inches in height), remove each seedling from its container without touching the stem. Cut away the container if necessary. Dig a hole in your vegetable bed; place the seedling in the hole, keeping the top of the soil even with the soil of the bed; and gently press the garden bed soil around the seedling.

Program Instructions: Setting up the Vegetable Frame for Winter

- **Step 1:** "Amend" your vegetable garden bed a minimum of 10 days to 2 weeks before transplanting the seedlings to it. Amendments can include adding organic compost and/or organic seaweed fertilizer and organic chicken/poultry manure to the soil of the bed and then watering these materials in. Microbial activity decreases when the temperature drops, and this affects how plants grow and take up nutrients. You want to provide the plants with nutrients and have them take root and start growing before the first frost arrives. As long as the temperature remains above freezing at night (i.e., before the first frost), you can continue to fertilize lightly once you transplant—not more than once a week. Stop fertilizing once the first frost arrives.

- **Step 2:** For a quick and simple garden bed setup, wire garden hoops, frost cloth, and something to hold down the frost cloth will be all you need. The main function of the hoop tunnel is to keep the frost cloth off the plants but be small enough for the space it encloses to warm up during the day and thus create a "greenhouse" for your plants.

- Set up the wire garden hoops (to form a tunnel) in the bed before you transplant. Some wire hoops are sturdy enough to push into the ground without needing anything additional to steady them. If you purchase wire garden hoops that have "eyes" on either side, you will need to purchase rope and stakes. Thread the rope through the eyes from one hoop to the next, staking the rope ends down on either side of the bed. This will help stabilize the hoops. Both PVC and metal hoops are also available. Whatever you choose, the hoops must be high enough to accommodate your greens at full size, usually about two feet above the soil. Leaving less room up top will help create a warmer greenhouse for your vegetables.

- Lastly, your frost cloth will go over the wire hoops (like an awning) and be held down at its edges by rocks, bricks, or boards. There are two things to keep in mind when purchasing frost cloth: temperature and the amount of light that can penetrate the cloth. You will want to protect your plants from the lowest temperature reached in your garden: if in winter, your yard never goes below 15 degrees F, then you will want your frost cloth to protect to 10 degrees F or colder, just to be safe. Any frost cloth should allow enough light to penetrate into your created greenhouse if it is indeed frost cloth—and not another type of cover, like plastic or a sheet. Frost cloth will also allow the penetration of rain and snow to water your plants without having to be removed. For snow, just leave it piled on the frost cloth and let it melt through to water the plants.

- Watering your plants will depend on how cold and wet your winters are. Water in the late morning or early afternoon and water at the base of the plants, avoiding the leaves if possible. For warmer winters, you can lay a soaker hose in the bed before transplanting, with the open end of the hose sticking out from under the frost cloth. This way, if you have not had moisture and it's warm enough to water, you can attach the hose to the open end of the soaker hose without removing the frost cloth. For colder winters, if you don't receive enough natural moisture, you will need to remove the frost cloth on warmer days and water by hand, with either a hose or a watering can.

RECOMMENDED NEXT PROJECTS

Now that you know how to grow seedlings, you can also grow them for your spring garden and offer a program specifically about growing seedlings for vegetable gardening. You can also experiment with branching out to growing herbs and edible flower seedlings, and even growing trees, shrubs, annuals, and perennials for yards from seed.

Growing Culinary Mushrooms

ROSE SIMPSON

I n this project, patrons will be introduced to growing edible mush-rooms, which requires a very different technique from growing leafy plants.* While there are several methods to grow mushrooms (such as on hardwood logs or in self-contained tubs), growing them in a bag of fortified growing medium like sawdust or straw is the easiest place to start. This project uses recycled newspaper pellets as the growing medium and requires no prior knowledge or specialized tools to produce impressive results. In 2-4 weeks, your patrons can have a fresh crop of tasty oyster mushrooms to use in their favorite recipes.

Age Range	Library Types	Cost Estimate
Kids (ages 3-7) [with parental assistance] Tweens (ages 8-12) Young adults (ages 13-18) Adults	Public and school libraries	$60-$90

*This program was originally created by Austin Larkin, a library aide at the New Haven (CT) Free Public Library.

FIGURE 3.1 | A successful crop of mushrooms

Cost Considerations

The cost may vary, based on the supplier for your mushroom grain spawn. The cost will also increase if you purchase small spray bottles for patrons to mist their mushrooms at home as they grow.

OVERVIEW

Because this program will allow patrons to grow something at home, there will necessarily be two parts to it: first where they assemble their grow bags in the library, and second where they tend to the mushrooms at home. The first part will take no more than an hour, while the second part may take up to 4 weeks.

The first part of the program is fairly straightforward and mostly involves mixing everything together and packing it into bags, so this part may be facilitated by just one staff member. If you have young children or a larger group, you may want additional staff on hand to assist.

The number of people your program can accommodate will depend on how much mushroom grain spawn you purchase. One 6-pound bag of grain spawn will provide enough for about 20–22 grow bags, but if time permits, you may want to measure out the amount of grain spawn ahead of time before you set a final number for how many people may attend the program.

This program also works well as a take-home project kit to be completed independently. To make such a kit, portion out the mushroom grain spawn, newspaper pellets, and alfalfa pellets each into separate little bags, and then package them together with the newspaper bag, the printed instructions, and a spray bottle (optional). Provide this for each participant to take home. Participants can then mix the grain spawn and pellets together in the newspaper bag at home, add water, and start growing their mushrooms. Make sure patrons are aware that the water they use for this must be dechlorinated.

NECESSARY EQUIPMENT AND MATERIALS

- Oyster mushroom grain spawn
- Alfalfa pellets
- Newspaper pellets
- Newspaper bags
- Bins or bowls for mixing
- Dechlorinated tap water
- Measuring cups (1 cup and ½ cup)

Recommended but Optional Materials

- Small spray bottles
- Disposable tablecloths (filling the bags can get a little messy)

STEP-BY-STEP INSTRUCTIONS

Preparation

The recycled newspaper pellets are sold as cat litter. Look for Purina's "Yesterday's News" brand, specifically the unscented, softer-textured variety that comes in a purple bag. If you can't find it, finely shredded newspaper may also work.

Mushroom grain spawn consists of grains that have been colonized with mushroom spores. Look for a reputable company that sells this, such as North Spore. Because the grain spawn contains living organisms, its shelf life is limited, and the spores may either start to grow on their own or die if left unused for too long. Therefore, try to order the grain spawn so that it arrives no more than 2–3 weeks before your program. There are many varieties of oyster mushrooms (Italian, pink, golden, snow, blue, etc.), and any of them will work for this project.

Old newspaper bags are great to hold the mushroom-growing mixture because they're a good size, the bags are not treated with any antimicrobial chemicals (which could kill the mushrooms), and it allows the reuse of some plastic bags that are often considered trash.

The water used for this program must be dechlorinated because the chlorine in tap water can kill the mushrooms. To allow the chlorine to dissipate, either boil tap water for a few minutes and then let it cool to room temperature, or leave it out in an uncovered container overnight.

The program will run more smoothly if portions of supplies are measured out ahead of time. Each patron will need 4 cups of newspaper pellets, ½ cup of alfalfa pellets, 1 cup of mushroom grain spawn, and 4 cups of dechlorinated tap water. Each of these portions can be stored in individual bags or containers so that patrons can mix them together during the program.

Program Instructions

Part 1: In the Library

- Mix the newspaper pellets and dechlorinated water in the mixing bin (or bowl) and let them sit for 5–10 minutes until they absorb all the water.
- Stir the soaked mixture to fluff it up a little, and then add alfalfa pellets and the mushroom spawn.
- Mix well. The mixture should be just wet enough that when you squeeze a handful of it, a few drops of water drip out, but no more. Then use clean hands to fill each newspaper bag with this mixture.
- Gently pack down the mixture to remove air pockets, and then tie a knot at the open end of the bag.

Part 2: Growing at Home

- Cut four 1″ slits in the newspaper bag (which has already been filled with the mixture of newspaper pellets and grain spawn).

- Place the bag in a dark, cool area (60–70 degrees F).
- After 2–4 weeks, the bag should be filled with white mycelium, which looks like little threads winding through the growing medium. At this point, move the bag to a cool, well-lit room, but keep it out of direct sunlight.
- Inspect daily for signs of baby mushrooms (called primordia) growing at the slits or elsewhere. Cut more holes in the bag if necessary to free the growing mushrooms. Use dechlorinated water to mist the mushrooms several times a day, as evaporation stimulates growth, but do not soak or over-wet.
- If the growing medium gets too wet, mold may start to grow, which can contaminate or kill the mushrooms. Conversely, if the air is too dry, the growing medium may dry out too quickly.
  - If mold is caught early, gently remove the mold and continue growing. If the mold issue continues and the mushrooms die, the growing medium should be discarded.
  - If you find the growing medium drying too quickly, making a tent out of a plastic bag can help keep the air around the grow bag humid.
- The mushrooms should double in size every day. Pick whole clusters of them when each mushroom is about 2 inches in diameter.
- When all the mushrooms have been picked, return the bag to the cool, dark place to repeat the process. One bag has the potential to produce two or even three crops of mushrooms.
- When the bag stops producing mushrooms, it can be used to make a new bag. This will require more newspaper and alfalfa pellets, but patrons can break up the old bag's growing medium and use it in place of the grain spawn. The old growing medium is already full of mushroom mycelium, so it just needs new nutrients and a new bag to start growing again!

RECOMMENDED NEXT PROJECTS

Oyster mushrooms are the easiest mushrooms to grow and are widely recommended to beginners because they will reportedly grow on just about anything. For most other mushrooms, the growing medium must be sterilized before you inoculate it with mushroom spores. If your patrons develop an interest in mycology, you might consider presenting a program on sterilizing the growing medium and using it to grow another type of relatively easy-to-grow mushroom, such as lion's mane mushrooms. Be aware that sterilizing the growing medium may require more equipment, such as a pressure cooker.

Alternatively, fresh coffee grounds can be used for growing some types of mushrooms (because the grounds have been boiled to brew coffee, they are already sterilized). You can try partnering with local coffee stores to reuse their old coffee grounds for another program on growing mushrooms. Make sure to collect the grounds on the day of your program, as it's important that they're fresh.

Mason Jar Hydroponic Gardening

CELESTE TAPIA

H ydroponics is a method of growing plants without soil or some other traditional dirt medium and instead using a water solution that is rich in mineral nutrients. Plants can grow with their roots directly submerged in the mineral solution, or you can use perlite, gravel, or some other medium. Hydroponically grown foods not only taste better and are more nutritional, but you can change the properties of your food, monitor what goes into your food, and pollute less. You can also grow more food in less space. This is great for those who don't have a backyard or outdoor area to grow in. Weeds are eliminated in a hydroponic system, and pests are almost nonexistent.

Age Range	Library Type	Cost Estimate
Young adults (ages 13-18) Adults	Public libraries	The cost is about $10-$13 per hydroponic kit (a kit used to grow plants without soil); for a program of twenty kits, the price ranges from $200-$250.

FIGURE 4.1 | Completed Mason jar with new plant growth

OVERVIEW

In a traditional garden, plant roots have to seek out nutrients in the soil. In hydroponic gardens, nutrients are dissolved in the water that surrounds the roots, so plants have even easier access to the nutrition they need. Are you ready to grow your indoor garden? This program can be done as a "take-and-make" kit at home or at the library in two parts because the seeds need to grow a little bit prior to putting together the kit.

While this program was created for adults, it can easily be geared to tweens and teens with minimal supervision. Regular program staffing is more than adequate for this program, especially if the plants have already sprouted. Paired with books and additional information about home gardening, the presentation can easily take 45 minutes to an hour. Just running the program as listed, it will take some time for the seeds to sprout, but beyond that, putting everything together does not take very long. You can increase the session's length by having patrons decorate their Mason jars ahead of planting using paint pens, chalk paint, and so on.

NECESSARY EQUIPMENT AND MATERIALS

- 20 wide-mouth Mason jars
- 20 spray bottles
- 20 3-inch net pots
- 20 1-inch rockwool cubes

- 25-liter bag of hydroton clay pellets
- 20 seed packets
- 20 packets of plant fertilizer, such as Miracle Grow

Recommended but Optional Materials

- Scissors

STEP-BY-STEP INSTRUCTIONS

Preparation

1. Start off by washing your Mason jar and hydroton clay pellets. The clay pellets should be rinsed under the tap with a colander, but the Mason jar can go in the dishwasher if you want.
2. Remove the metal lid from your Mason jar, but don't throw it away. You will need the band later.
3. Test-fit your net pot so you're sure that it fits snugly into the Mason jar (the metal band should still screw onto the jar, clamping the net pot in place).
4. Put the rockwool cube in water, and then plant 6–8 seeds in it and wait for them to sprout. It's best not to mix seed types, for ease of labeling later. Every few days use the spray bottle to keep the rockwool wet. You don't need to soak it; just make sure it doesn't look dry.
5. Once your seeds have sprouted and you have roots coming out of the bottom of the cube, you can move on to the second part of the program.

Program Instructions

1. Follow the package directions for diluting your fertilizer. You don't want to over-fertilize your new plants because that could burn their roots.
2. Put your net pot into the top of the Mason jar, and then fill with your fertilizer and water mixture.
3. Put a layer of hydroton pellets, one pellet deep, at the bottom of the net pot. Put your rockwool cube (seedling up) into the pot, and then fill in the sides and top of the net pot with more hydroton pellets.
4. Set your net pot back snugly in the jar, and then screw on the jar's metal band to secure it in place.

5. Place your Mason jar in a spot where it will get plenty of light.
6. Enjoy watching your plant grow. Be sure to check the water level in the jar once a week or so as the plant grows so it doesn't dry up. When the water level gets low, fill the jar up about ¾ of the way full. Don't fill it up all the way to the net pot because you will drown your plant.

Remember to be creative. Perhaps you could add a layer of chalkboard paint on the jar. Or maybe you could paint in the name of the plant using some paint pens.

RECOMMENDED NEXT PROJECTS

A great next step, if you enjoyed this project, is to do it on a larger scale. You can make a balcony-sized hydroponic gardening kit, or you can set up a special hydroponic garden at your library. (There are great instructions at www.instructables.com/Urban-Gardening-Balcony-Hydroponics.) You can also work with local garden clubs or similar organizations to discuss making compost, best gardening techniques, and more.

Straw Bale Gardening

ELLYSSA KROSKI

S traw bale gardening is a simple and inexpensive way to grow all manner of vegetables, herbs, flowers, and even fruit. Like container gardening, the bales of straw require little space and can be placed just about anywhere. These versatile raised garden beds can be configured in a variety of layouts and designs and offer a perfect foundation for trellises and vertical gardening. In addition to providing a medium free from ground-dwelling pests, soil-related diseases, and most weeds, straw bales provide an elevated base, making this type of gardening appealing to growers of all ages and ranges of mobility.[1]

Libraries have been offering patrons gardening instruction and related workshops for many years, as well as developing seed collections and establishing community and teaching gardens for patron engagement. As the trend to sustainable living grows, libraries can continue to meet patron needs by offering innovative programming in the form of teaching straw bale gardening techniques. This chapter will walk librarians through the process of how to create a straw bale garden that they can relate to patrons through workshops or by creating and planting such a garden with them.

FIGURE 5.1 | A simple six-bale garden planted with lettuce, tomatoes, garlic, potatoes, onions, and carrots

Age Range	Library Types	Cost Estimate
Kids (ages 3-7) Tweens (ages 8-12) Young adults (ages 13-18) Adults	Public, academic, and school libraries	$50-$100

Cost Considerations

Straw bales can be acquired at your local feed and grain store and cost about $6 each. How many bales you purchase and how large a configuration you want to achieve, along with your seeds and/or starter plants, will determine your end cost. My six-bale garden cost me $36 plus the cost of a $13 soaker hose, fertilizers to condition the bales, planting soil, and seeds. I would also highly recommend the purchase of Joel Karsten's book *Straw Bale Gardens Complete* for $25, as he details the conditioning process for each day (from one to twelve) to get the bales ready for planting, as well as providing many other helpful tips.

OVERVIEW

This program could encompass either creating a community straw bale garden for and with library patrons, or inspiring them to create one themselves by means of an instructional workshop. Ancillary programming ideas might be to form a library gardening club around this project, which would take ownership of the straw bale garden and undertake regular maintenance of it. This program details how to set up a straw bale garden from scratch.

NECESSARY EQUIPMENT AND MATERIALS

- Straw bales
- Soaker hose(s)
- Nitrogen-rich lawn fertilizer (without weed killer)
- 10-10-10 fertilizer
- Planting soil
- Vegetable, fruit, herb, or flower seeds and/or seedling plants

Recommended but Optional Materials

- Karsten, J. 2019. *Straw Bale Gardens Complete: Breakthrough Method for Growing Vegetables Anywhere, Earlier and with No Weeding.* Beverly, MA: Cool Springs Press.

STEP-BY-STEP INSTRUCTIONS

Preparation

Decide where you will put your straw bales. They need lots of sun (6+ hours a day) plus water, so you will probably want to place them in a sunny spot by a spigot so that you can run your soaker hose to them easily. Count on buying your bales about 2 weeks before you'll begin planting so that you can condition them in the correct way before the planting season begins. This is also a great time to order your seeds or purchase them at a local store. I'm a little adventurous, so I order mine from Baker Creek Heirloom Seeds, which offers seeds from around the world (at www.rareseeds.com).

Their annual 500+ page *Whole Seed Catalog* would be a wonderful purchase for a library collection or gardening club.

Librarians who are unfamiliar with gardening can begin by finding their planting zone on a map such as the USDA's "Plant Hardiness Zone Map" at https://planthardiness.ars.usda.gov. This will give you a starting point for finding out what plants grow well in your area of the country and when to plant them. You can then search online for a planting calendar for your zone. I would also highly recommend locating the closest cooperative extension program for your county. These organizations work together with Master Gardeners who can provide advice about local planting, pest control, and more on their website. The extension program is also a valuable source of local speakers for the library. You can find your local extension cooperative by entering your zip code here: www.gardeningknowhow .com/extension-search.

Consider at this time if you will need a fence around your straw bale garden. Not only do I have an inordinate number of rabbits on my property, but my goats will eat just about anything they can get their hooves on. I use metal garden fence posts and plastic webbed fencing in order to enclose my straw bales and keep them free from uninvited guests. They are sturdy materials that I am able to reuse every year.

Program Instructions

- Purchase your straw bales from the local feed and grain store or nursery and be sure to ask for "wheat straw." When first starting out, I mistakenly bought pine straw, which is not at all the same density and quickly collapses when you try to work with it. Also avoid hay bales, which look almost exactly the same as straw bales. Hay bales are full of seeds that unfortunately will start growing into your garden.
- Arrange your straw bales in whatever configuration you'd like, bearing in mind that you may want to construct a trellis along one side for heavier plants like tomatoes or those that respond well to vertical gardening techniques such as cucumbers, squash, beans, and sugar snap peas. I would recommend following online tutorials or Karsten's instructions for creating a trellis with a combination of wood and metal garden posts, with wire or string run taut between them for a trellis.

My first year I purchased a metal trellis from my local hardware store to lean/attach a tomato plant I had grown in the bales from seed. The plant grew to enormous proportions in the bale, and the trellis was not nearly sturdy enough to support it.

When arranging the bales, you'll want to place them on their sides so that the narrower side of the bale is resting on the ground. This seems counterintuitive because you want as much planting surface as possible, but placing them on their sides not only gets the bales further off the ground, but the strings hold the bale together (these strings should now be visible on either side of the bale) and will help it keep its shape once you start gardening in it.

- Condition the bales. There are many straw bale conditioning schedules that are freely available online. However, I prefer Karsten's schedule, which he clearly explains in his book. His schedule involves spreading a ½ cup of lawn fertilizer on the top of each bale every other day, and then spraying the tops of the bales with the hose to sink the fertilizer into them. On the "off days" the bales are merely watered; after the first day, Karsten recommends using warm water in order to saturate the bales and thus speed up the "cooking" process that makes the bales decompose. Toward the end of the schedule, specifically days 7–9, you reduce the lawn fertilizer to a quarter cup per bale, along with warm water. On day 10 you will switch to using 10-10-10 fertilizer at one whole cup per bale, along with a saturating hose spray. Day 11 is a rest day and nothing need be done, followed by planting day on day 12. In sum, this is his schedule:

Day 1	½ cup lawn fertilizer per bale, spray with hose to saturate.
Day 2	Water bales with warm water.
Day 3	½ cup lawn fertilizer per bale, water bales with warm water.
Day 4	Water bales with warm water.
Day 5	½ cup lawn fertilizer per bale, water bales with warm water.
Day 6	Water bales with warm water.
Days 7, 8, 9	¼ cup lawn fertilizer per bale, water bales with warm water.
Day 10	1 cup 10-10-10 fertilizer per bale, water with hose.
Day 11	Rest day.
Day 12	Planting day.[2]

ONE HINT that I will mention about this process is that your straw bales will become quite smelly about halfway through, and this is how you know the conditioning process is working. In essence, by "conditioning" your bales, you're making them decompose and rot to become a nice composted material in which to plant. Another tip is that you may notice mushrooms either during the conditioning process or soon afterward. Again, this is normal. I just ignore them, as I don't know whether they are edible or not.

- Set up your soaker hose(s). Arrange your soaker hose right down the center of the bales and stake it in with some garden or landscape staples.
- Plant your bales. This is the long-awaited planting day, and you are ready to go. You can place seeds directly into the bales, but my preference is to lay Miracle-Gro Garden Soil for Vegetables and Herbs and then plant seeds in that, allowing the roots to grow down into the bale. You can lay your soil alongside the soaker hose or right underneath it and plant the seeds nearby. Some people spread their soil before staking down the soaker hoses, or else they spread it just in the spots where they'll be planting seeds. If you're transplanting seedlings or starter plants, you will want to dig into the bale and transplant them directly into the bale.

  Consider your planting area as more than just a flat surface (i.e., the top of the bale). You can plant relatively deep into the bale with potato and onion starters, while also planting a short-harvest, surface-oriented plant such as lettuce shallowly on the bale's top. I have had success with doing this, as well as "bedazzling" my bales with flowering ground-cover coming out of the bales' sides.
- Water the plantings daily and maintain them as you would a regular garden.
- Replant. You can usually get at least two plantings out of the same bales, such as an early spring crop of lettuce and peas, and then tomatoes and cucumbers in the late spring or summer. Your bales may even be firm enough for an autumn harvest.

- Deconstruct the bales. At the end of the season, you will end up with a fantastic compost material that you can add to flower beds or other gardens.

RECOMMENDED NEXT PROJECTS

After you've mastered the straw bale garden, you can continue your program by hosting related programming such as composting with the remains, starting a library garden club, or instructional workshops.

NOTES

1. LayLa Burgess, "Straw Bale Gardening Factsheet," Clemson University Cooperative Extension Service, August 1, 2017, https://hgic.clemson.edu/factsheet/straw-bale-gardening/.
2. Joel Karsten, *Straw Bale Gardens Complete: Breakthrough Method for Growing Vegetables Anywhere, Earlier and with No Weeding* (Beverly, MA: Cool Springs Press, 2019).

PART II
Preservation Programs

Hands-on Canning Workshop
The Basics of Pickling

KATE McCARTY

C ome learn the process of making your own pickled vegetables and preserving them for year-round enjoyment through canning. This hands-on food preservation workshop taught by UMaine Extension volunteers and staff will teach you the basic steps for pickling vegetables and for canning using the boiling water bath process. Learn the basics such as preserving equipment, recommended recipes, and specialty ingredients. Enjoy the satisfaction and great flavor that come from pickling fresh vegetables. Participants will make a batch of pickles, learn the steps in canning, and each take home a jar of pickles.

Age Range	Library Types	Cost Estimate
Young adults (ages 13–18) Adults	Public and school libraries	$50–$75

Cost Considerations

The costs for this workshop can be reduced if you solicit donations or grocery store gift cards. Ideally, the workshop is provided free of charge in order to increase participant access.

OVERVIEW

In this 2½-hour workshop, participants will learn how to make cucumber pickles and how to can using the boiling water bath canning process. Canning is a process that creates a shelf-stable product that is best eaten within one year of canning. Participants will learn the basics of canning and pickling as they prepare cucumber dill pickles for canning. Everyone will go home with a jar of pickles to enjoy, as well as the skills necessary for canning other in-season foods, like tomatoes and apples. This program is best taught by 2 people and limited to 15 participants.

NECESSARY EQUIPMENT AND MATERIALS

- A kitchen facility with room for participants to work:
  - Large sink and stove or 2 electric burners
  - Potable water
  - Handwashing sink
  - Tables and a chair for each participant
  - Table for check-in materials, instructor materials, and handouts

- A boiling water bath canner. Options include:
  - A boiling water bath canner
  - A Ball Freshtech Electric Water Bath Canner
  - A large pot with a rack in the bottom, i.e., a lobster pot or corn steamer, that is deep enough to hold enough water to cover pint jars by 1–2 inches of water

- Canning tools: jar lifter, funnel, headspace measurer
- 16-ounce canning jars, including dome lid and screw band (1 per participant)
- Stockpot (at least 12 quarts)
- Sharp knives and cutting boards (1 per participant)

- Colander
- 5 large bowls (for washed and prepared vegetables)
- 2 small bowls (for vegetable waste)
- Digital timer
- Potholders
- Large, sturdy cooling rack
- Teaspoon set
- Large liquid measuring cup and dry measuring cups
- Ladle
- Paper towels
- Permanent marker
- Recipe ingredients: pickling cucumbers (2–3 per person, 15 pounds total); 128 ounces of white vinegar (5 percent acidity); 1 box of pickling and canning salt; granulated sugar; 2–3 heads of garlic (1 clove per participant); and spices: dried dill seed, dried dill weed, or fresh dill seed heads; yellow mustard seed, whole mixed pickling spice
- Sponge or dishrag and dish soap, dish towels, dish-drying rack or mat
- A packet of fact sheets on pickling and canning (1 per participant) (See the Resources list later in this chapter.)

STEP-BY-STEP INSTRUCTIONS

Preparation

- Review the USDA's *Complete Guide to Home Canning* available at: https://nchfp.uga.edu/publications/publications_usda.html; and the University of Maine's Cooperative Extension Bulletins #4079 "Let's Preserve: Steps to Success in Home Canning," #4078 "Let's Preserve: Food Canning Basics," and #4044 "Let's Preserve: Pickles." (See the Resources list later in this chapter.)
- Wash hands thoroughly and begin with a clean kitchen environment.
- One hour before the program starts, fill the boiling water bath canner (with a rack in the bottom) about two-thirds full of water. Make sure a pint jar can be fully submerged in the water. Wash the canning jars, lids, and screw bands. Preheat the jars by placing the jars upright in the canner, fully submerged, so the jars are full of water. Bring the water in the canner to a simmer over medium heat on the stove or electric

burner. Preheating the jars will help reduce the chance of jars breaking when they are filled later in the program. Set the clean lids and screw bands in a bowl next to the canner.

- Place the stockpot on the stove. On a clean work surface nearby, put out vinegar, liquid measuring cup, salt, and dry measuring cup.
- Place one cutting board and one knife where each participant will be working.
- Place one packet of pickling information and any promotional materials you plan to mention at the beginning or end of your program where each participant will sit.
- Collect the library's available food preservation resources and place them on a table in the room where the program will be held.

Background Information for the Instructors

- Review the basics of using a boiling water bath canner to preserve pickled cucumbers. This process involves submerging specialty canning jars, filled with brine and vegetables and capped with the two-part metal dome lid and screw band, into simmering water. You then bring the water in the canner to a boil and begin timing the boiling, as specified in your canning recipe (10 minutes for pints of quick fresh-pack dill pickles if you're at an elevation of less than 1,000 feet). After 10 minutes of boiling, turn the heat off, remove the canner lid, and let the jars cool for 5 minutes in the warm water. The boiling process destroys any molds, yeast, and bacteria inside the jars because they cannot survive temperatures above 212 degrees F. Boiling for 10 minutes ensures every spot inside the jar is heated thoroughly to 212 degrees F. The heating and subsequent cooling of the jars produces a vacuum seal, which seals the lid onto the jar and makes it shelf-stable for up to one year. Pickling occurs after canning as the flavor of the vinegar, salt, and spices infuses the vegetables. Pickles should sit for 4 to 5 weeks to allow flavors to develop fully.
- The boiling water bath method of canning can also be used to can jams, jellies, relish, salsa, and some tomato products. A pressure canner is needed to preserve vegetables and meats. Review the basics of canning in the USDA's *Complete Guide to Home Canning*, "Guide 1: Principles

of Home Canning." This will give you a thorough understanding of the process and ensure that you are comfortable explaining to participants how thermal processing destroys molds, yeasts, and bacteria and creates a vacuum seal.

- Note that a boiling water bath canner can hold only 8 or 9 one-pint jars, so if your program participants exceed that number, you will have to either use two canners or can two batches of pickles separately. Be sure to build in the additional time if you plan to do two batches. You can also choose to limit the program to 8 participants.

- Your local land-grant university's cooperative extension is a great resource for no- and low-cost instruction if you're not comfortable delivering the program yourself.

Program Instructions

- Begin by welcoming participants to the program. Introduce yourself and any staff or volunteers assisting you with the program. Explain how long the program will last and what participants can expect. I also say that we will be seated and listening for a bit and then up and working in the kitchen area on the preserving project.

- Explain how canning works, why you need to can food using a boiling water bath, and when a pressure canner is required. Explain how quick-pickling vegetables with vinegar adds flavor as well as acidity, making boiling water bath canning a safe way to preserve pickled vegetables.

- Explain the equipment needed, demonstrating with items where appropriate (i.e., canning jars, canning tools, a jar of previously canned pickles). Review the process of filling a jar, including using the jar lifter, jar funnel, and headspace measuring tool for participants.

- Review the Quick Fresh Pack Dill Pickles recipe from the University of Maine's Cooperative Extension Bulletin #4044, "Let's Preserve: Pickles," with the group. Review the different participant roles and stations that you set up before class (washing and preparing the cucumbers, preparing brine, peeling garlic).

Recipe Instructions

- Instruct 1–2 participants on how to create pickle brine by combining vinegar, water, sugar, and salt in the stockpot. Bring the mixture to a boil, and then reduce the heat to medium-low and keep it warm. (Don't let it boil for too long or it will evaporate, and then you won't have enough brine for all participants.)

- Instruct the remaining participants to wash and trim the cucumbers. One-sixteenth of an inch of the blossom end of each cucumber needs to be removed to prevent enzymes present in it from causing soft pickles. The cucumbers also need to be trimmed so they will fit into a pint jar. Provide a clean pint jar for participants to check that the vegetables will fit in the jar with a ½-inch headspace. Pickles require a ½-inch headspace, so be sure to explain headspace in your introduction.

- When the brine and vegetables are prepared, begin filling the jars with them for canning. Add vegetables along with garlic cloves and spices, and then cover these with brine. Remove air bubbles by using the other end of the headspace measurer. Measure the ½-inch headspace, adjust as needed by adding or removing brine, and then wipe the rim of each jar with a clean paper towel. Apply the dome lid and screw band until they are fingertip tight. Demonstrate filling one jar, and then let each participant fill their own jar with vegetables, brine, and spices according to the recipe. Label each lid with a participant's initials so participants can retrieve their own jars after the canning process is complete.

- Once the canner is full of filled jars, apply the lid, and bring the water to a boil. As previously described, you should process the pints of pickles in the boiling water bath canner for 10 minutes, adjusting for altitude as needed. Once 10 minutes have elapsed, turn off the heat, remove the lid, and let the pickles sit in water for 5 minutes. Then remove the jars from the canner with a jar lifter and place them on a cooling rack. Let them cool for the remainder of the class.

- If the jars seal before class ends, show participants the difference between a sealed jar and an unsealed one by comparing the lids on the two jars. The button in the middle of an unsealed jar remains popped up, while a sealed jar will be concave, as the button is pulled in by the vacuum. Review the proper procedure for the aftercare of

CHAPTER 6: Hands-on Canning Workshop

the jars: let them cool, undisturbed, for 12 to 24 hours after canning. Once cool, check that vacuum seals have formed, and then remove the screw bands for storage. Label and date the jars and store them in a cool (50–70 degrees F), dark, dry place.

- Instruct participants to refrigerate the pickles once they are home. Canning requires that the jars sit, undisturbed, for 12 to 24 hours after heat processing for proper vacuum seals to form. Because participants are taking jars home instead of letting the jars cool properly, USDA guidance means that the jars should be refrigerated for safety. Advise participants to let the pickles stand for at least a week before eating in order to allow their flavor to develop, and to eat the pickles within 2 weeks of opening a jar (for safety).
- You may choose to have participants complete an evaluation of the program.

RESOURCES

Use these resources to compile a packet for participants:

- University of Maine Cooperative Extension Bulletins:
  - Bulletin #4033, "Let's Preserve: Refrigerator Spring Pickles," https://extension.umaine.edu/publications/4033e/
  - Bulletin #4044, "Let's Preserve: Pickles," https://extension.umaine.edu/publications/4044e/
  - Bulletin #4078, "Let's Preserve: Food Canning Basics," https://extension.umaine.edu/publications/4078e/
  - Bulletin #4079, "Let's Preserve: Steps to Success in Home Canning," https://extension.umaine.edu/publications/wp-content/uploads/sites/52/2015/04/4079.pdf
  - Bulletin #4273, "Using Home-Preserved Food Safely," https://extension.umaine.edu/publications/4273e/
  - Bulletin #4277, "Can Home-Canned Food Spoil?," https://extension.umaine.edu/publications/4277e/
  - Bulletin #4381, "Canning Fruits and Tomatoes in a Boiling-Water-Bath Canner," https://extension.umaine.edu/publications/4381e/
  - Bulletin #4382, "Canning Vegetables in a Pressure Canner," https://extension.umaine.edu/publications/4382e/

- Bulletin #4383, "Freezing Fruits," https://extension.umaine.edu/publications/4383e/
- Bulletin #4384, "Freezing Vegetables," https://extension.umaine.edu/publications/4384e/

- You can also provide information on how to connect with the National Center for Home Food Preservation (at homefoodprervation.com) or its cookbook, *So Easy to Preserve.*

RECOMMENDED NEXT PROJECTS

If your canning program goes well, you might consider offering workshops for making other preserved products using the boiling water bath method, like jams, salsa, or applesauce. You can also offer programs on other methods of food preservation like pressure canning, dehydrating, and fermenting.

Fermentation 101
How to Make Sauerkraut

ELIZABETH PEIRCE

From yogurt to sourdough, soy sauce, beer, wine, and kombucha, fermented food and drinks are all around us. Many people are tuning into the benefits of probiotics (found in fermented food) for the health of our gut flora and are seeking an inexpensive alternative to probiotic supplements. Then there are the foodies who love the rich, earthy flavors of ferments like sauerkraut—one of the most popular and easy-to-make fermented foods. With a few basic tools and ingredients, you can help program participants make their own jar of kraut to ferment at home. It's a satisfyingly hands-on process that older kids and adults alike will enjoy.

Age Range	Library Types	Cost Estimate
(Kids should be old enough to safely use a sharp knife; could be done with adult supervision) Tweens (ages 8-12) Young adults (ages 13-18) Adults	Public and school libraries (that have a demo kitchen)	Cost: $85 (without tools) to $235 (including tools)

Cost Considerations

Here's a cost breakdown for the ingredients you'll need to make sauerkraut, along with the jars that participants will take home.

- 12 one-liter-size wide-mouth Mason or Ball jars: $35
- 10 cabbages at $2 per head: $20
- 1-lb. box of kosher or pickling salt: $3
- Box of small Ziploc bags (to fill with water and use as weights): $3
- *Optional extra ingredients:* A few beets, a couple of red cabbages, ginger root, garlic, leeks or shallots, a bottle of juniper berries, a bottle of caraway seed, and a bottle of dill weed: $25

Here's a cost breakdown for tools, if your library doesn't have them. (Prices were obtained from the Walmart website):

- Cutting boards: $5 × 10 = $50
- Chef knife: $3 × 10 = $30
- Glass (or plastic, but not metal) mixing bowl: $6 × 10 = $60
- Measuring spoons (2 sets to share): $2.50 × 2 = $5
- Tools total = $145

FIGURE 7.1 | Bottles of sauerkraut made at the Halifax Public Library ready to begin fermenting

OVERVIEW

This program is ideally suited to a group of 6 to 12 participants, with 1 to 2 staff members present to supervise. You will be modeling the chopping of the cabbage, mixing it with salt in a bowl, and then packing it into jars. A 90-minute program should allow enough time for all the steps to be completed. Allowing at least 30 additional minutes for cleanup time is really important, as things can get a bit messy. Participants can wipe down their work stations, but the equipment will need to be washed and floors swept.

NECESSARY EQUIPMENT AND MATERIALS

- 1-liter size wide-mouth Mason or Ball jars
- Small to medium-size cabbages (green)
- Box of kosher or pickling salt
- Box of small Ziploc bags
- Cutting boards
- Chef knives or paring knives
- Glass or plastic mixing bowls (not metal, as it can interfere with the fermentation process)
- Measuring spoons
- Water

Recommended but Optional Materials

- Dark red beets (to add color to the kraut)
- Ginger root
- Juniper berries
- Caraway seeds
- Dill weed
- Red cabbage
- Garlic
- Leeks or shallots
- Cheese grater (for grating beets and ginger root)

STEP-BY-STEP INSTRUCTIONS

Preparation

If your library has a copy of Sandor Katz's marvelous book *Wild Fermentation*, I would bring it to the program room and recommend it highly as a resource for all kinds of fermenting projects.

The recipe for sauerkraut is super simple, but if you'd like to print enough copies of Katz's basic recipe for participants to use or take home, it can be found at www.wildfermentation.com/making-sauerkraut-2.

Before participants arrive, set up the work stations with a cutting board, knife, bowl, and cabbage for each participant, along with a jar and a Ziploc bag. Set up a communal table with a box of salt, spices, measuring spoons, and optional ingredients participants can choose from. A clean, wet cloth at each table is a good idea too.

Once they arrive, explain to participants the three basic tasks you'll be doing together: chopping the cabbage, mixing it with salt, and packing it into a jar. You'll also want to explain that the actual fermenting part will happen at their house over the next 3 days to several weeks. The longer the cabbage ferments, the more sour its flavor will be—remind them to taste-test their kraut every few days to find the right level of pucker for their taste.

You should also remind them that fermenting is a very safe and natural process and won't make them sick if they make a mistake. The important part is to keep the vegetable below the liquid in the jar so it can ferment optimally.

Program Instructions

Wash the cabbage well in cold water, and finely chop or shred it. The finer it is, the easier it will be to draw the juices out of the cabbage; the cabbage will be submerged in these juices. (Note that a 2-pound cabbage, chopped or shredded, will fit into a 1-liter jar.) Wash and chop or grate any desired additions to the kraut: grated ginger, shredded beet, chopped shallots, garlic, or leeks.

Mix the shredded cabbage and any additions with about 1 tablespoon of salt using clean hands—really squeeze the cabbage, which will release more of the juices.

Pack the cabbage into a clean jar, using your hands or a soup ladle to press down hard on the vegetable, allowing juices to float to the top. Don't fill the jar all the way to the top.

Each participant should fill their Ziploc bag with water and seal it tightly. Press the bag down on top of the cabbage to ensure it stays below the brine (the bag of water acts as a weight—in bigger batches of kraut made in a crock, a scrubbed rock sitting on a dinner plate is sometimes used for this purpose).

Screw the lid on each jar, reminding participants that the lactic acid bacteria that activate the fermentation process don't need oxygen to survive. Once they take their jar home, it should sit on a countertop at room temperature—and it's important to open the lid each day, especially in the first few days, to release carbon dioxide and taste the kraut. Sauerkraut ferments quickly in a warm environment; move the jar to your fridge when the desired degree of sourness is reached—this will slow down the fermentation process and keep the kraut fresh for several months. Encourage participants to enjoy taste-testing the kraut at various stages of fermentation, and also remind them that sauerkraut juice or brine makes an excellent digestive aid.

Troubleshooting

A potential "yuck" factor in fermentation is the white scum that sometimes forms on top of the liquid—these are yeasts and molds and are the result of contact with oxygen. Remind participants that this is normal and that the scum can be safely scraped off the top and discarded, along with any discolored vegetable near the top. A little bit of scum will remain in the brine—that's okay. The kraut below the surface is fine to eat.

RECOMMENDED NEXT PROJECTS

Want to go a step further in your food-preserving journey? Why not grow your own vegetables at home? I can show you how: visit my website at elizabethpeirce.ca. Here you'll find links to my kitchen and garden self-help books, as well as my online food gardening course, Sprout, where you'll learn everything you need to know to start (or expand) your organic veggie garden, from starting seeds to troubleshooting common problems (pests, weeds, and more). Hope to see you there.

How to Make Lilac Syrup

KRISTIN WHITE

W hat's more sustainable than taking a cutting from a tree and then turning it into something as yummy and unique as a simple syrup? With this program, you will not only draw an audience of people interested in homesteading, but also one of flower gardeners and people looking to try something new. By offering this program, you can also incorporate a trip outdoors to collect lilac blossoms. And the best part about this program is that lilacs are in bloom almost everywhere. It makes for a great spring program and gift-giving idea. Lilacs are easy to identify but don't always last long when cut. One way to preserve their beauty is to make syrup from the petals. This is a cost-effective, unusual program that can easily be adapted to other florals and foraged items.

Age Range	Library Type	Cost Estimate
Adults	Public libraries	$0–$100, depending on the number of participants and how many jars will need to be purchased

FIGURE 8.1 | The finished product: lilac syrup

OVERVIEW

With this project, there are opportunities to learn about cooking and using unusual ingredients. Time is of the essence, though, as lilacs usually only bloom in the spring and for a short window of time. You will want to identify your lilac bushes beforehand if you haven't already. Alternatively, you can have participants bring their own lilac blossoms if there aren't any lilac bushes available near the library. You will want to pick only those blooms that are fresh, and avoid any dying blossoms. You will need at least 2 cups of blossoms for this project, so that will require a considerable number of lilac cuttings. The ratio for this recipe is 2 parts lilac blossoms to 1 part sugar water.

There are many creative uses for lilac syrup, and here are a few suggestions:

- Add it to lemonade or tea or some other favorite beverage.
- Add it to baked goods.
- Add it to icing for a cake.

Be sure to advise participants that this is a simple syrup, and it will add an extra sweetness to whatever it's used in. It's also a good idea to remember that when using it in baked goods or in icing, some of the other liquids will need to be decreased to accommodate the simple syrup.

You should allot at least 90 minutes for this program. The longest portion of the program will be allowing for the steeping of the blossoms. This program is considered a cooking program, so the participation size should be kept small to ensure that participants can follow along at a reasonable pace and to allow for different prep and cook times. Please note that the color of the finished product will be a light brown.

NECESSARY EQUIPMENT AND MATERIALS

- Kitchen shears for cutting lilac blooms
- Kitchen strainer
- Stock pot or pan with lid
- Water
- Sugar
- Cheesecloth
- Spoon
- Bowl
- Pint jar with lid
- Stove top or hot plates
- Pens or markers for marking date on jars

STEP-BY-STEP INSTRUCTIONS

Preparation

- Identify the lilac bush that will be used.
- Collect lilac blossoms by cutting the stems bearing them from the bush.
- Once you have the lilac cuttings, instruct participants to pick the florets (small blossoms) off the stems by pulling them off in a downward motion over a kitchen strainer.
- After the florets have been removed, rinse them under cold water. Encourage participants to pick through the florets and pull out any unnecessary detritus as possible.

Ingredients

- 1 cup of granulated sugar
- 1 cup of water
- 2 cups of tightly packed lilac blossoms

Program Instructions

- Bring the sugar and water to a boil in a medium saucepan over medium heat, stirring every few minutes.

- Turn heat to low and simmer for 5 minutes, and then remove from heat and cool for 10 minutes.
- Add the lilac blossoms to the sugar water pot. Stir gently to combine.
- Place the lid on the pot and let the mixture infuse until cooled. Advise participants that if they are making this at home, they will want to take care to not let the mixture infuse for longer than 3 hours, as the sugar in the syrup combined with the heat can speed-start the decomposition process of the flowers.
- Place a strainer lined with cheesecloth over a large bowl and pour the syrup and lilac mixture into it, straining out the blossoms.
- Pour the syrup into clean glass containers and seal tightly.
- Mark the date on the container.
- Refrigerate the syrup, for up to 2 weeks. Be sure to check for spoilage before using.
- Compost the blossoms in your compost bin.
- Yield: 1 pint

RECOMMENDED NEXT PROJECTS

- A great next program would be herbal infusions. Instead of making simple syrup, participants would infuse oils, such as olive oil, with herbs and/or flowers.
- You could also consider a cooking program that uses simple syrups.

Preserving Foods through Dehydration

MARIA PORTELOS-ROMETO

ood dehydration is one of the oldest forms of food preservation. Dehydration, simply put, removes moisture from the food item in order to prevent the growth of spoilage and microorganisms that can cause illness. Dehydrating foods can be simple and easy. The food is placed in a food dehydrator, which circulates hot air that reduces the moisture content of the food. The dehydration process also reduces bulk so that the food item becomes lightweight. Dehydrated food can be great for taking on trips, hiking, snacking, used in soups, stews and casseroles, and so on. Because it prolongs the food's shelf life, and the food's nutrient content is concentrated, it is a wonderful alternative method of food preservation.

In this program students will learn which foods dehydrate easily and basic kitchen skills such as properly preparing the food item, knife skills, food safety, and proper storage.

Age Range	Library Types	Cost Estimate
Tweens (ages 8–12) Young adults (ages 13–18) Adults	Public, academic, and school libraries	$100–$500

Cost Considerations

- The cost depends on the choice of food dehydrator used.
- Supplies such as cutting board, kitchen knives, jars or storage containers, and kitchen cleaning items.

OVERVIEW

In this project, students will learn the basics of preserving food through dehydration. The program's length depends on what food items will be dehydrated. Vegetables and fruits can take up to 15 hours to dehydrate, depending on the quantity and the food selection. The program can be an hour in length to discuss food preservation and demonstrate how to prepare the food item to prevent spoilage, as well as cutting the fruit or vegetable to place on the dehydrator tray. The project brings awareness to sustainable practices by demonstrating one method of food preservation.

NECESSARY EQUIPMENT AND MATERIALS

- Food dehydrator
- Cutting board(s)
- Kitchen knives
- Storage containers
- Cleanup supplies such as dish detergent

STEP-BY-STEP INSTRUCTIONS

Preparation

Preparing Food for Dehydration

- Before beginning, all fruits and/or vegetables must be thoroughly washed, with some food requiring peeling.
- Cut the food items into uniform pieces about ⅛ to ¼ inch thick.

There are four methods to prevent food from spoiling prior to dehydration:

1. Blanching (i.e., steaming or boiling in water):

- Steam blanching of fruit to stop enzyme production; the blanching also retains color and slows oxidation
- Boiling water blanching for vegetables; it also retains color and stops enzyme production
- Syrup blanching used for fruits

2. Antioxidant dips: Follow the directions on the package, or soak the cut fruit in a fruit juice high in ascorbic acid or vitamin C.
3. Cooking: This is for pureed fruits and vegetables that are made into leathers (i.e., dehydrated fruit products).
4. Sulfuring: Sulfur dips are effective, but this method is not recommended due to allergic reactions in some individuals, and it can corrode metal parts of the dehydrator.

Program Instructions

Drying Procedures

- Arrange the pre-treated, cut food in single layers on trays.
- Remember, the pieces should not touch one another.
- Place the trays in the food dehydrator. Follow the drying times for specific foods. Drying times can vary from 3 hours to 15 hours.
- As the food items are drying, it might be necessary to reposition the trays to achieve uniform drying.

Testing for Dryness

- Fruits: should be pliable but not sticky
- Vegetables: leathery or brittle
- Fruit and vegetable leathers: should easily peel away from the tray and be a bit chewy

Preparing Food for Storage

- Place the cooled, dried food in a glass or plastic container no more than ⅔ full and cover tightly.

- Shake the contents daily for about 7 to 10 days to detect any moisture and/or spoilage.
- If moisture condensation appears, return the food items to the drying trays for further drying in the dehydrator.
- Discard food that has mold or other signs of spoilage.

Packing and Storing

- Pack the food item as soon as it has cooled completely.
- For best results, pack the items in glass jars such as ½-pint canning jars, or you can use food-grade plastic freezer containers.
- For fruit or vegetable leathers, pack them in parchment paper and place them in a plastic bag that seals tightly.
- You can also choose to vacuum-pack the food item for excellent results.
- Store the food in a dark, cool, dry place.
- Food stored at 60 degrees Fahrenheit or below will keep for 1 year.
- Food stored between 80 to 90 degrees Fahrenheit will begin to deteriorate within several months.
- Consider freezing the food for longer storage.

RECOMMENDED NEXT PROJECTS

Once dehydrating fruits and vegetables is mastered, the next program could be to master dehydrating meats and making jerky.

Making Herbal Tea Blends
A Hands-on Program about Common Herbs and Their Uses

MARTHA NAPOLITAN COWNAP

n this program participants will smell, taste, and learn about various tea herbs and make some into tea bags that they can take home. Easy-to-grow medicinal and flavorful herbs will be on hand, as well as a handout about their traditional uses.

Age Range	Library Types	Cost Estimate
Tweens (ages 8–12) Young adults (ages 13–18) Adults	Public and school libraries	$50–$100

OVERVIEW

Growing and using herbs is a delicious, healthy, and sustainable hobby. In this hour-long program, a jar of each dried herb will be passed around while you describe its uses and growth habits. (Fresh herbs can also be used.) Participants will get to taste and smell each herb, and they can take a bit to make into a tea bag. The number of participants will be limited by the supplies and tables, but 10–15 is a good number.

NECESSARY EQUIPMENT AND MATERIALS

- A variety of dried, loose tea herbs in pint- or quart-sized glass jars. About 1–2 ounces of each herb will be plenty for a group of 15. Try to get least 4 different herbs. Some suggestions are: mint, chamomile, lemon balm, tulsi, catnip, stevia leaves, dandelion leaves, nettle leaves, lemon verbena, hibiscus, and rose petals. Many health food stores sell loose, dried herbs.
- Empty, drawstring-style paper tea bags, size small (about 2 × 3 cm). These can be ordered online. Order early because they can be difficult to find in stores.
- Teaspoons: 1 per type of tea herb
- Paper plate, pencil, and paper lunch bag (1 of each per participant)
- Tables and chairs
- Books on herbs, with photos of the herbs you will be using

Recommended but Optional Materials

- A pot or 2 of hot tea that you have made, and cups
- Fresh sprigs of the herbs, or the plants themselves, if available

STEP-BY-STEP INSTRUCTIONS

Preparation

- Buy or gather the materials listed above.
- Learn something to tell about each herb, or find a short written description that you can read aloud while each herb is being passed around.
- Set a paper plate, pencil, and 4–6 empty drawstring tea bags at each place.
- At your table, set up the labeled jars of herbs, any plants or sprigs you have, and the books about herbs.

- (*Optional*): Make a 1-sheet handout about the herbs you will be using, and make a copy for each participant. Below is a sample of what you might say on the handout. You are welcome to use these descriptions (which are written for herbs that are easily grown in most temperate climates).
  - *Mint*: Both spearmint and peppermint are perennial herbs. (They stay alive for years even though the top part of the plant dies back in winter.) They make a lovely, uplifting tea, either fresh or dried. Mint is invigorating, but it won't keep you awake the way caffeine does. A strong, cold, mint tea taken in small sips can relieve nausea. It is also good for clearing the sinuses and cures some types of headaches. Spearmint and peppermint have similar effects, but peppermint is stronger.
  - *Tulsi:* Also known as holy basil, this is an annual plant related to basil that is sacred in parts of India. It is widely used in Ayurvedic medicine for both physical and emotional well-being. Tulsi tea helps people to relax and concentrate, so it is often used before people meditate or take exams. It has also been shown to help normalize blood pressure. Tulsi is an annual plant in our climate, so it must be planted every year.
  - *Chamomile:* This flower has been used for thousands of years for its effects of calming the nerves and easing upset stomachs. A very gentle sleep aid, it is a perfect tea to give to children who have had a stressful day. Some people with PMS or menstrual cramps find some relief from drinking chamomile tea.
  - *Pine needles:* A tea made of pine needles is used for respiratory health. It is good for colds and coughs, and it is high in vitamin C. Just make sure it is really from a pine tree and not the needles of the poisonous yew.
  - *Stevia:* Stevia is a South American plant that is fairly easy to grow here as an annual. The leaves are very sweet, and it can be added to other herbs to give sweetness without calories.
  - *Lemon balm:* Many people enjoy the uplifting lemon-peel scent of lemon balm. It is an easy-to-grow perennial and makes a relaxing after-dinner tea. A strong infusion of lemon balm helps cold sores to heal more quickly.

- (*Optional*): Make a pot or 2 of some or the teas that you will be using so participants can try them.

Program Instructions

- Welcome everyone and describe what you will do. Pass out the handout if you made one.
- One herb at a time, pass around the open jars of herbs, with a spoon in each one. While an herb is being passed around, participants can each take a spoonful and put it on their paper plate. Encourage them to smell it and admire it. Tell them something about the herb or read a short passage about it as it is being passed around. If they want, they can write the name of the herb on the paper plate next to the herb.
- (*Optional*) If you have made a tea of a particular herb, you can serve it while that herb is being passed around and described.
- After all the jars have been passed around and described, and each person has taken a bit of each, then everyone can fill their empty tea bags. (If you are doing this with children, pass out the tea bags last.) They can either make blends or keep the teas separate. To fill the tea bags, they can just use their fingers and tie the bag shut with an overhand knot.
- At the end of the program, they can put their tea bags into the paper lunch bags to take home and browse the library books about herbs that you have displayed.

RECOMMENDED NEXT PROJECTS

- Tour a local herb garden.
- Learn how to grow your own herbs.

You're Sup-herb!
An Introduction to Herbal Medicine

VELYA JANCZ-URBAN and EHRIS URBAN

I n this program participants will learn how to benefit their health by making two herbal remedies: a "knock your socks off" herbal heating pad and an "evening repose" herbal infusion. Many people are interested in herbal medicine, but they're overwhelmed with how to start, and they think they're going to harm themselves and their families without guidance. They stare longingly at the bulk herb bins in health food stores, but because the bins only list the SKU, price per pound, and the herb's Latin name, it's hard to know how much of the herb to buy and what to do with it. This program's hands-on approach aims to increase participants' confidence in, and knowledge of, the use of herbs for healing. Through this program, participants will begin to celebrate and deepen their connection with medicinal herbs, learn how to support their health by making their own natural remedies, and whet their appetites for further holistic exploration.

Age Range	Library Types	Cost Estimate
Young adults (ages 13–18) Adults	Public and school libraries	$150 for 30 participants (we suggest that participants provide their own sock)

OVERVIEW

In the "knock your socks off" herbal heating pad workshop, participants will learn how to create a DIY herbal heating pad using a simple sock. This simple herbal remedy is useful for helping relieve migraines, menstrual cramps, muscle aches and backaches, and warming up on a chilly day.

The "evening repose" herbal infusion program walks participants through how to create a loose-leaf herbal infusion blend that will make about 16 cups of tea. Nervine-rich, this blend is relaxing, helps relieve stress and anxiety, and may help you achieve a restful sleep. Nervines—like chamomile, skullcap, and catnip—nourish the nervous system and help to relieve stress and anxiety.

FIGURE 11.1 | A medicinal herb garden

NECESSARY EQUIPMENT AND MATERIALS

"Knock Your Socks Off" Herbal Heating Pad

- Sock: 1 per participant (knee sock or tube sock)
- Uncooked rice: about 2 cups per participant (enough to fill ¾ of a sock)
- Dried herbs
  - Ginger
  - Clove
  - Lavender

  - Rosemary
  - Spearmint
  - Allspice

- Measuring cups and spoons
- *Optional*: cotton string

Evening Repose Herbal Infusion

- Dried herbs
  - Chamomile flower
  - Skullcap leaf

  - Catnip leaf
  - Alfalfa leaf

- Measuring spoons

FIGURE 11.2 | A green witch herbal workshop

- Paper bags, Ziploc bags, or wax paper bags to store the herbal infusion blend
- Labels

STEP-BY-STEP INSTRUCTIONS

Preparation for "Knock Your Socks Off" Herbal Heating Pad

The benefits of the herbs used here may be described in a handout prepared ahead of time and/or discussed at the beginning of the workshop:

- **Ginger** (*Zingiber officinale*): Warming and decongesting, ginger is an effective (and tasty) remedy for menstrual cramps, PMS, nausea, motion sickness, seasickness, circulation issues, respiratory congestion, colds, and flu.
- **Cloves** (*Syzygium aromaticum*) have traditionally been used for a variety of purposes, including as an analgesic (pain reliever) and natural anti-inflammatory.
- **Lavender** (*Lavandula angustifolia*) is a well-known relaxing herb. It's helpful for nervous exhaustion, anxiety, stress, and disturbed sleep.
- **Rosemary** (*Salvia rosmarinus*): Many people use rosemary only as a seasoning on their roasted potatoes or roasted chicken. Little do they know that rosemary can be made into an herbal infusion. It tastes kind of minty and is helpful for anxiety, depression, exhaustion, and insomnia.
- **Spearmint** (*Mentha spicata*) renews, energizes, and refreshes without depleting or using up energy reserves.
- **Allspice** (*Pimenta dioica*): Maybe we're the only ones who didn't know this, but allspice is made from the dried berries of *Pimenta diocia*, which is a member of the myrtle family. We thought it was a blend of cinnamon, cloves, and nutmeg.

Program Instructions

1. Pour uncooked rice into the sock until it's about ¾ full. You want to leave room to be able to tie the sock closed at the end.
2. To the rice-filled sock, add:
    - 2 tablespoons of dried chopped ginger root

- 8 cloves
- ⅓ cup of dried lavender flowers
- ¼ cup of dried rosemary leaves
- ¼ cup of dried spearmint leaves
- 1 teaspoon of allspice powder

3. Tie a knot in the sock, or tie it closed with cotton string.
4. To use: microwave the sock for 1 minute. If additional heat is desired, the sock can be microwaved for an additional minute.
   - While we generally don't advocate the use of microwave ovens, for this purpose, it's okay. If, like us, you choose not to own or use a microwave, the sock can be placed in an oven-safe dish in a 200 degrees F oven for 15 minutes.
   - Conversely, this heating pad can be placed in the freezer and used as a cold "ice pack."
5. Once the sock is heated or cooled, apply it to the affected area of your body. If the sock is too hot, let it cool, or wrap it in a cloth before using. Be careful if you're using the sock heating pad on an area of your body where you don't have as much feeling, and avoid numb areas. If you can't feel the heat as strongly, you might not realize if you burn yourself.
6. This heating pad can be reused over and over.

Preparation for Evening Repose Herbal Infusion

The benefits of the herbs used here may be described in a handout prepared ahead of time and/or discussed at the beginning of the workshop:

- **Chamomile** (*Matricaria chamomilla*): Many people hold their tension, stress, or worry in the stomach or solar plexus area—and after a while, all that "junk" accumulates. Chamomile helps to release this tension and promotes calm and serenity.
- **Skullcap** (*Scutellaria lateriflora*) has traditionally been used to help quiet the mind, treat insomnia, and ease anxiety and irritability.
- **Catnip** (*Nepeta cataria*)—calming for humans—has the totally opposite effect on cats. For humans, catnip soothes the nerves, relaxes tension, and relieves stress.
- **Alfalfa** (*Medicago sativa*): "Alfalfa? Isn't that what they feed cows, horses, and rabbits?" A tonic herb, alfalfa contains one of the highest

chlorophyll content of any land plant. Alfalfa may help support the heart, ease menstrual/menopause symptoms, and alleviate allergies. It's been known to send its roots almost 50 feet underground to reach nutrients it can't get on the surface. *Don't use alfalfa in combination with blood thinners.*

Program Instructions

1. To each paper or Ziploc bag, add ¼ cup of chamomile, 3 tablespoons of skullcap, 3 tablespoons of catnip, and 2 tablespoons of alfalfa. Mix to combine.
2. Label the bag with contents and instructions.
3. To prepare a cup of evening repose herbal infusion:
   - Place 2 teaspoons of the herb blend in a tea ball or tea infuser and place it in a mug.
   - Pour 1 cup of boiling water into the mug, over the herbs.
   - Cover the mug with a saucer (this is important—covering your mug ensures that the herbs' volatile oils and benefits stay in the mug, and don't evaporate into the air) and steep for 10–15 minutes.
   - Strain, add sweetener if desired (honey, agave, stevia), and enjoy!

RECOMMENDED NEXT PROJECTS

After this program, libraries might want to continue offering herb-related workshops, such as the one discussed in the previous chapter: "Making Herbal Tea Blends."

Ehris Urban, Velya Jancz-Urban, and Grounded Goodwife, LLC are not responsible for the use or misuse of these herbs, ingredients, practices, or recipes. Like all medicines, plants and holistic practices may be dangerous if used or performed improperly, and the authors do not endorse or guarantee the curative effects of these subjects or recipes. The practices discussed in these recipes are the lifestyle choices of the authors and may not be for everyone. If you have any physical or mental health issues or are taking any prescriptions/medications, you may want to keep your health care professional in the loop about your holistic undertakings and herbal supplements.

PART III
Pioneer Crafts Programs

Repair Events in Libraries
Sharing Fixing Skills and Fostering Sustainable Culture

GABRIELLE GRIFFIS

R epair events are a hands-on intergenerational community activity in which people bring their broken items to be guided by repair coaches who will (hopefully) fix their defective things. At a repair event, participants will learn fixing skills, connect with fellow community members, and help keep items out of the landfill. Repair events help foster a culture based in social and environmental stewardship by providing a space where people can preserve resources and consider the cost of manufacturing and the impact of waste.

Age Range	Library Types	Cost Estimate
Kids (ages 3–7) Tweens (ages 8–12) Young adults (ages 13–18) Adults	Public, school, and academic libraries	$0–$500

Cost Considerations

Repair event budgets vary widely. They can be held with no money, relying on volunteers and donated resources, or on a much larger budget if a library wants to invest in tools and other resources. Typically, refreshments are provided at repair events, and this should also be considered.

OVERVIEW

Repair events can be small or large depending on the venue space and coordinating capacity. Programs are typically 3 hours long, with 1 hour before and after for setup and cleanup. Small pop-up repair events can be held with repair experts for specific items such as bikes or sewing machines, or can be larger with repair coaches who specialize in different items. Partnering with organizations such as local schools, recycling committees, conservation committees, and other groups can help to delegate responsibilities and broaden outreach. Recruiting repair coaches should be done at least 2 months in advance of the program. A meeting should be held in advance with the coaches to go over the objectives of the repair event and the tools that will be brought by the volunteers, or provided by the library. At the repair event itself, participants will bring their broken items to the library to be guided by a repair coach on how to troubleshoot, disassemble, and hopefully fix their malfunctioning things.

NECESSARY EQUIPMENT AND MATERIALS

- Electrical outlets and extension cords
- Assorted batteries
- Check-in table
- Intake and exit forms
- Signage
- iFixit Pro Tech Toolkit
- Needle-nose pliers
- General hand tool set
- Scissors
- Dremel tool
- Clamps

- Goggles
- Drill and drill bits
- Guitar picks or old credit cards for prying items open
- Rubbing alcohol: 91 percent isopropyl
- Contact cleaner spray
- Clean toothbrushes, rags, Q-tips, and paint brushes for cleaning
- Soldering kit
- Glues and other adhesives: superglue
- Lubricants: WD-40, lithium grease
- Various colored permanent markers
- Compressed air
- Emery board, files, sandpaper
- Assorted tapes: duct tape

Recommended but Optional Materials

- Name tags or repair coach T-shirts
- Aprons for tools
- A bell or buzzer to announce a repair
- Refreshments
- 3-D printer to create irreplaceable parts

STEP-BY-STEP INSTRUCTIONS

Preparation

- Decide what type of repair event will be hosted and what it will be called. Organizers can call the program a "Repair Event" or can use the name and free resources provided by organizations such as Repair Cafe and Fixit Clinic available on their websites.
- Assess the available program space to determine the size of the repair event, including an inventory of electrical outlets. Smaller libraries can host pop-up repair events or host events outside if the weather permits.
- Determine the program's budget. Repair events can be organized with little to no money, or with a lot of money for tools and refreshments. Repair coaches often bring their own tools, but having tools available is also very useful.

- Find cosponsors such as local schools, conservation or recycling committees, makerspaces, and so on. Cosponsors are not necessary, but having a team to coordinate the event will make planning and execution easier.
- Determine the duration of the event. Repair events are typically 3 hours long, with 1 hour for setup and 1 hour for cleanup.
- Delegate responsibilities such as publicity, repair coach coordinator, refreshments, setup, cleanup, greeting, tool inventory, event documentation and social media (such as taking pictures with consent), and so on.
- Recruit the repair coaches. Recruitment should start at least 2 months in advance. Recruitment can be done through flyers, press, and social media announcements, and asking prospective coaches directly, as well as by word of mouth. Flyers should contain the date of the repair event and be specific about the fixing skills that are needed.
- Advertise the repair event starting at least 1 month in advance of the program. Flyers, press releases, social media posts, and PSAs on local television and radio stations are great ways to get the news out. The specific types of repair services being offered can be advertised in the flyers, such as general repair, electronics, jewelry, household appliances, book mending, sewing, and so on.
- A meeting with the repair coaches should be held 1 to 2 weeks in advance of the actual event in order to go over objectives, tool inventories, and expectations. The repair coach coordinator should emphasize that a major point of the repair event is to teach fixing skills to participants. Participants should be the ones handling and fixing their broken items, and be guided by the coach through the process—rather than the repair coach doing the manual labor.
- The setup for the repair event should be done at least 1 hour before the program, with tables, chairs, electrical outlets, extension cords, tools, signage, greeting tables, refreshments, and so on. A waiting area of a few chairs can help with event traffic flow if all the repair coaches are occupied.

Program Instructions

- When the repair event begins, greeters at the entrance should be stationed to welcome participants, hand out intake and exit forms, explain the event's expectations and objectives, and direct people where to go. Greeters can also take exit forms when participants leave.
- Having volunteers to oversee refreshments and having someone to take pictures, with consent, can be very helpful. Having a bell or buzzer to announce a repair is a fun way to get everyone involved.
- After the program, organizers should handle the intake and exit forms. Anonymous information about the types of repairs handled can be useful to share with right-to-repair organizers such as Fixit Clinic.
- Event photos can be shared to social media with appropriate permission. Press releases can be written to local papers. Thank-you cards should be written and sent to all repair coaches and volunteers.

RECOMMENDED NEXT PROJECTS

Creating a tool library at your library can be a great resource for the community and for future repair events. Repair events focused on mending specific items such as clothing or bicycles can be a great way to teach concentrated fixing skills.

13

Steps to Sustainable Grab & Go Kits

LAUREN ANTOLINO, MARISSA LIEBERMAN, and
VERONIQUE PAILLARD-BAUMANN

G rab & go kits (or "grab-and-go bags") have become increasingly popular since the start of the pandemic, when patrons could not come into the library building, and they have continued in popularity even when library doors have opened again because of the convenience and innovation each new kit provides. Many libraries are still providing grab & go kits on a regular basis for different age groups, and staff have to consider not only the grab & go project itself, but also the materials being provided and the overall packaging. After reading this chapter, you will learn how to incorporate more sustainable products and concepts in grab & go kits, as well as how to make a wallpaper gift bag kit for adults.

Age Range	Library Type	Cost Estimate
Adults	Public libraries	$0–$150

FIGURE 13.1 | A sustainable wallpaper gift bag grab & go kit

Cost Considerations

Your budget will depend on the amount of supplies you are able to reclaim and reuse. When you create a cost-effective project using secondhand materials, you can always reallocate funds toward more expensive, locally sourced materials for other projects. For example, one of our monthly kits includes reusing a surplus of old library catalog cards to make a sewing needle holder. This project costs nothing. The money saved from this project will be allocated to purchasing wire from a local wire manufacturer to make wire heart decorations for another month's grab & go kit.

OVERVIEW

When creating sustainable grab & go projects, it is important to keep the kit's packaging as minimal as possible. You can house kits in paper bags, use recycled paper like card catalog cards to create simple envelopes for small supplies, and favor projects that don't require plastic or items that will end up in the landfill.

The best way to ensure that your project materials are sustainable is to start with what you already own. Consider ways to use supplies that you have lying around or items that can easily be collected from staff members and the community. Check with local manufacturers for donations of items like paint, fabric, or wallpaper samples. When purchasing your supplies, choose natural materials and things that can be recycled. If your budget permits, buy locally sourced and durable materials. Reach out to your Friends of the Library group for support and partnership.

Our journey for reusable supplies led us to a local trade showroom that was getting rid of old books of wallpaper samples. And don't forget to check your library's basement. We found a book of vintage wallpaper samples in ours. Read on to learn how to create a sustainable wallpaper gift bag grab & go project

NECESSARY EQUIPMENT AND MATERIALS

- 2 pieces of wallpaper samples
- Gift bag template
- Scissors or X-Acto knife (not provided)
- Ruler (not provided)
- Glue (not provided)

STEP-BY-STEP INSTRUCTIONS

Preparation

For assembling wallpaper gift bag kits, visit https://bit.ly/3EuoWId to access the template, project photos, and written instructions for this project. Start by printing the template onto a sheet of 11 × 17″ paper. Cut the sheets of wallpaper into 9 × 18″ pieces. Pack 2 sheets of wallpaper and the template into a paper bag. Staple the instructions to the front of the kit.

Program Instructions

For assembling the wallpaper gift bag, librarians can provide the following instructions to patrons:

- Cut your template and place it on one of the wallpaper pieces, leaving a 2-inch strip of wallpaper that you will use to create a handle and tags.
- Find the markings on your template. Cut along the straight lines and fold along the dotted lines.

- Shape the bag by folding the creases inward.
- Tuck the extra side flap in, sandwiching the small bottom pieces between the large ones. Apply glue where needed.
- Use the wallpaper that you put to the side in step 1 to create a 2 × 8″ handle. Fold the strip in half, lengthwise, and glue it. For a better finish, lay your piece on the wrong side, draw a line in its center, lengthwise, and bring the edges toward the center line. Once dried, glue the handle to the interior of the gift bag.
- Repeat with the other piece of wallpaper.

RECOMMENDED NEXT PROJECTS

- Make a sewing needle holder using a folded card catalog card and felt, preferably made of wool.
- Reuse clothespins to make a trivet, a necklace, and a bracelet.
- Make wire bookmarks or decorative ornaments.

14

How to Make Rolled Beeswax Candles
A Family-Friendly Program to Light Up Your Day

JENNIFER GARGIULO and CELESTE TAPIA

Rolled beeswax candles are an easy and fun way to introduce patrons to sustainable programming. This project can be done in the library but is simple enough that, if necessary or desired, it can be completed 100 percent from home.

AGE RANGE

While this program is geared toward adults, it can also be appropriate for tweens and young adults independently, and for kids with adult supervision. It works great as an intergenerational program.

- Kids (ages 3–7)
- Tweens (ages 8–12)
- Young adults (ages 13–18)
- Adults

Library Types	Cost Estimate
Public and school libraries	$30–$50

FIGURE 14.1 | Participants creating their own beeswax candles

Cost Considerations

The above costs are estimated based on twenty participants in a virtual take-and-make program. The only materials included in the take-and-make were the beeswax sheets and cotton wicks, but for an in-person program, purchasing craft mats or utility knives might be required. Scissors and rulers are not included in the supply costs, as these are standard office supplies.

OVERVIEW

In this 1-hour project, participants will learn how to make rolled beeswax candles. While learning how to do the project, they will also learn about the sustainability options with regard to the candles. For example, once the candle has burned down, the wax can be remelted into another candle or used as a lip or skin balm.

This program can be managed in a variety of ways, depending on the audience. If the targeted audience is adults, more participants can be managed by one staff member. For an in-person live program of this sort, the maximum number of participants can be determined by staffing and the materials budget.

If the targeted audience is tweens or teens, more supervision may be required, and it is recommended to cap the program at 10 participants. Intergenerational or family programming will likely require an extra staff member, but each librarian knows their community best, so staffing for a standard craft program will most likely be adequate. For an intergenerational live family program, a cap of 5 or 6 families is recommended.

NECESSARY EQUIPMENT AND MATERIALS

- Cotton wick
- Beeswax sheets (color optional but encouraged)
- Craft mat or cutting board
- Ruler
- Scissors
- Pizza cutter or utility knife
- Hair dryer to gently warm the wax if necessary

Optional Materials

- Washi tape
- Ribbon
- Other decorative materials
- Cardboard or wood squares to act as a base

STEP-BY-STEP INSTRUCTIONS

Preparation

Before beginning this program, set aside 15 minutes for setup. Make sure that there is a clean work surface. When setting out materials, you might find that you don't have enough scissors, rulers, cutting mats, and so on for each participant to have their own. In this case, group the materials together so that a similar number of participants are sharing each set of tools.

Start with a review of the materials to ensure that each participant has what they need. Cutting mats, rulers, and scissors are often shared and can dictate the size of the group of participants. From there, the staff member should go through the instructions for the pillar candle, helping participants along the way. Once the pillar candle is created, the staff member demonstrates the tapered candle. Once all demonstrations are completed, participants are free to make as many candles as supplies allow.

Program Instructions

For pillar candles:

- Using the pizza cutter or utility knife, cut a beeswax sheet in half, making two pieces about 4 × 4¼".
- Cut the wick about ½" longer than each beeswax sheet, using the scissors.
- Lay the wick along the edge of the sheet and start rolling the candle by bending over about ⅛" of the wax, leaving the extra ½" of wick for the top of the candle.
- Press tightly to secure the wick. This is the only time you will press really hard.
- As you begin to roll, gently apply pressure as you push the rolled candle forward. Make sure to use even pressure so that both ends of the candle are straight and even.
- Continue until you reach the end of the wax sheet, and gently press the edge into the candle.
- When you are done use, apply light pressure to make sure the candle is round, but be careful not to press too hard, which might damage the honeycomb pattern.
- Decorate the candle as desired, and press it into a base. (The decorations can be other colored beeswax, ribbon, washi tape, etc.)
- Trim the wick to ¼" before lighting.

For tapered candles:

- Cut a beeswax sheet in half diagonally.
- Cut the wick about ½" longer than the beeswax sheet.
- Place the sheet in front of you so that the right angle is in front of you and to your right-hand side.
- Follow the directions for the pillar candle, making sure to roll tightly so that there are no air pockets.

Please note that the sizes of the beeswax sheets are recommendations; using sheets with different dimensions will produce different and unique candles.

RECOMMENDED NEXT PROJECTS

Once this program has been mastered, a great next project (which is also sustainable) for your participants is making teacup candles by using thrifted teacups, cotton wicks, and melted beeswax. Participants can also go further with the rolled candle project by creating designs out of other colored beeswax to adhere to the candles they have made. Lastly, participants can learn how to make a beeswax-based lip balm or hand salve, which is a great use for their melted candle wax.

Upcycled Jewelry
Sustainable Programming for Teens and Adults

COLLEEN ELLITHORPE

Most libraries offer a wide variety of crafting and DIY programs, whether in person, remotely, or grab and go. As the library sector shifts to sustainable practices, upcycling is a fantastic way to offer crafting programs without contributing to throwaway culture. Unlike recycling, which breaks down materials to be remade into a new product, upcycling maintains the original item but refashions it for a different (and valuable) use. Upcycling is inherently budget-friendly because using donated or thrifted materials costs very little. The library is a natural place to educate and explore upcycling potential with community members.

Making upcycled jewelry is a low-cost, high-value program that can work in nearly any public library setting. Whether repairing a broken piece of jewelry or creating something new and unique, crafters of all ages will come together for the opportunity to learn a new skill and bring home a piece of jewelry they will cherish. Using donated or thrifted costume jewelry, this is an upcycling program you can offer again and again. And you don't need to be a fantastic crafter or jewelry repair expert to facilitate an upcycled jewelry program; anyone with a little practice and preparation can lead this program for teens, adults, and seniors.

Age Range	Library Type	Cost Estimate
Adults/seniors College students Teens	Public libraries	$0–$50

OVERVIEW

To prepare for an upcycled jewelry event, the facilitator will need to have a rudimentary idea of how to make basic jewelry. If the facilitator has no prior knowledge about this, they should start with jewelry tutorials, checking out some books, and most importantly, trying to upcycle jewelry themselves. It doesn't have to be pretty, but you'll want to be aware of how the jewelry pliers work, how to thread beads, how to use jump rings and use bead tips. If you have a friend, family member, or colleague who can coach you, that would be fantastic, but the basics are not hard to learn by oneself. Use your experience to prepare a digital presentation or slideshow for your program. Note what helped you, what didn't, and add that to the presentation. The facilitator doesn't have to be an expert on making jewelry; they just need to know the basics and be able to share them with the group during the event. Hands-on experience will also show you how long your upcycled jewelry program needs to be. It is safe to say that you will need 1.5–2 hours for this event. Participants will want to complete an item to bring home, but that may not always be possible. Remind participants that they are here to learn a new skill, and they may have to finish their project at home. If your library has a "Library of Things" collection, consider purchasing an extra set of pliers or a jewelry kit before your upcycled jewelry program.

When promoting upcycled jewelry, encourage patrons to bring their own pieces of broken jewelry, giving them an opportunity to fix something old or mix and match to create something new. Note that fine jewelry should be repaired or refashioned by a skilled craftsperson. This program is an event for costume jewelry and not for items of real or sentimental value.

Registration is necessary and is based on the number of materials you collect or purchase, as well as how many facilitators will be participating. If there is only one facilitator, limit the group to a number the facilitator thinks they can manage. In my experiences, I led the programs myself and limited the attendance to 10 participants. During the event, the facilitator should periodically "check in" with participants and try to assist them. The facilitator will be busy, so if your library can provide more than one facilitator, then you can consider expanding the registration.

When sourcing costume jewelry prior to the event, ask colleagues for donations first. You may be surprised at how many people want to get rid of their old costume jewelry. When sorting your donations, your focus should be on beads that can be reused. Look for long necklaces with 50 or more beads on them. Your donations may not always be pristine. You should discard or not accept items that are dirty or rusty. Earring hooks should be purchased new for sanitary reasons. It's also much easier to purchase new jump rings and bead tips than to try to use old ones. These materials can be purchased widely online for $5–$10. This initial investment can be used over a series of upcycled jewelry events.

When donations dry up, try a thrift store or yard sale to boost your inventory. You'll want a wide selection of items for participants.

When your upcycled jewelry program begins, start with a brief introduction. Tell participants that the goal is to learn a new crafting skill. Talk a little bit about your own crafting experience, and remind them that fine jewelry should be repaired or repurposed by a professional. Go over your presentation slideshow and pass around your upcycled jewelry examples. Show them any books you have assembled on the topic and encourage them to be open-minded.

After the initial presentation, have participants choose a few items with many beads to break apart. Participants can mix and match beads they like and start threading them on a length of fishing line or jewelry wire to make a new item. Some highlights of your presentation should include how pliers work, how to thread beads, how to use jump rings, and how to use bead tips to finish an item like an earring. It is useful to have visuals of these in your presentation. Many people will bring their own stashes of costume jewelry with the intent of sharing and swapping. Swapping is encouraged as long as there is no real or sentimental value to an item. If your space has the capabilities, play some music in the background to keep things lively.

NECESSARY EQUIPMENT AND MATERIALS

- Screen to play the presentation
- Costume jewelry
- Jewelry pliers
- Jewelry wire, fishing line, earring hooks, jump rings, and bead tips

Recommended but Optional Materials

- Crafting or jewelry books
- Snacks and beverages
- Background music

STEP-BY-STEP INSTRUCTIONS

Preparation

Pre-Event

- Ask colleagues for costume jewelry donations or visit a thrift shop or yard sale.
- Borrow or purchase jewelry pliers and fishing line, jewelry wire, jump rings, earring hooks, and bead tips.
- Prepare a few examples of upcycled jewelry items.

Day of Event

- Set up enough tables in your space for attendees to spread out and have their own areas.
- Create a "shared materials" area with donated costume jewelry, pliers, fishing line, and so on.
- Create a book display using your library's collection of relevant crafting books and materials and a list of relevant digital crafting resources your library may offer (like CreativeBug).
- Play music in your space and set up packaged snacks and/or drinks if permitted.
- Prepare the digital presentation.

Program Instructions

- A great way to get the group started is to show them some examples of upcycled jewelry. This can be on the slideshow, or you can pass examples around. This helps spark imagination and creativity.
- The facilitator may not be an expert in upcycling jewelry, but should make the rounds and try to assist participants.
- If someone is having difficulty or becomes frustrated, suggest taking a break and have a snack or beverage.
- If there is a more experienced jewelry upcycler among your group, encourage them to help others if they feel inclined.

Outcomes

- Participants will be able to bring home a repaired or "new" item (or more) of jewelry.
- Participants will have learned a new skill.

RECOMMENDED NEXT PROJECTS

- CreativeBug: "Found Necklace," www.creativebug.com/classseries/single/found-necklace
- UpCycle That! "Upcycling Ideas and Inspiration," www.upcyclethat.com/
- YouTube: "Upcycle and Repurpose Old Jewelry" videos, www.youtube.com/playlist?list=PLiTswRYlH_etWD3MpdyKlGQa81eSDxcHW or https://tinyurl.com/bdf7344s
- For more ideas on upcycled cycled jewelry programs, see https://programminglibrarian.org/blog/creating-upcycled-jewelry-program.

The Surprising Power of Hand Sewing

Use a Rugged Old Skill to Mend, Extend, and Uptrend Clothes and Accessories

ELLEN LUMPKIN BROWN

T his fun program transforms an essential pioneer craft into a powerful skill for modern, sustainable (and fashionable) living today. Hand sewing is a humble, practical art. With just a little practice and a few simple supplies, you can present an introductory session to your patrons that is brimming with discovery. At one time, everything from clothing to wagon covers was sewn by hand. Nowadays, there is a new appreciation for the value, beauty, mindfulness, and ethical rationale around hand stitching. Such a program is enjoyable, economical, and portable and requires minimal storage space. The program is especially good for young patrons, and participants will learn an impressive array of uses for the simple, straight-running stitch. At the end of the workshop, patrons will be familiar with how to repair, patch, embellish, and extend the life of clothes and accessories. This brief guide will provide everything needed to offer a memorable and exciting program and a skill that will last a lifetime, step by step.

Age Range	Library Types	Cost Estimate
Tweens (ages 8–12) Young adults (ages 13–18) Adults	Public and school libraries	$100–$300, depending on the supplies you may already have

OVERVIEW

This program introduces patrons to the magic and power of sewing by hand by making their own stitch sampler collection packet, with samples of various kinds of stitches. The key to this program is working on a small scale to teach the sewing techniques so that patrons can complete each learning project from start to finish. Once taught, the principles can later be applied at home or on the go. The program consists of demonstrations followed by hands-on work by patrons. I've included tips for a smooth and successful experience throughout this guide. A hand-sewing workshop lends itself to an intimate number of patrons of 10 or up to 15 with an assistant. Because the program involves a series of demonstrations that are immediately replicated by the patrons, an easy, clear line of sight is essential.

NECESSARY EQUIPMENT AND MATERIALS

A space with good light, comfortable chairs, and 1 or 2 table(s), although tweens and teens may want to sit on the floor.

For Librarian

- A patron hand-sewing kit
- A few stretchy, slippery, and dry-clean-only fabric scraps
- A finished patching sampler

For Patrons

(High-quality tools and equipment matter, so when you're purchasing the items listed below, you'll want to bear this in mind.) Each patron will need a hand-sewing kit consisting of the following items:

FIGURE 16.1 | A hand-sewing workshop

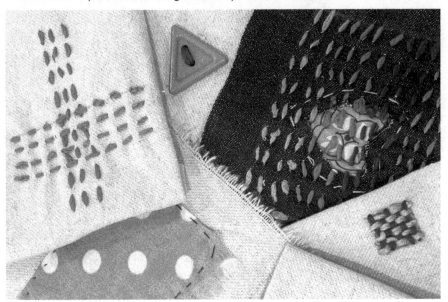

- Sturdy, long-eye embroidery needles 2 inches in length: 5 per patron
- Sturdy needle threader: 1 per patron
- 1 regular chenille needle: 1 per patron
- Ruler: 1 per patron
- Pencil: 1 per patron
- Large plastic buttons in fun shapes: 1 per patron
- 5 or so pins and a pincushion: 1 per patron (pins and needles can be put in the cushion)
- 6 six-inch squares of heavy muslin for each patron
- Fabric scissors: 1 pair per patron
- Baskets or other reusable (pioneer-style) receptacles for the patron kits
- A sturdy envelope for each patron to take their sampler home

To Share

- Spools of pearl cotton thread in several colors and weights, or craft cord like the kind used for friendship bracelets (you may already have this on hand)

- Scraps of lightweight, woven quilting cotton and a couple of inappropriate stretchy, slippery, or dry-cleanable scraps of fabric
- Spools of all-purpose white thread (use high-quality thread; bargain thread frays and breaks)
- Extra muslin squares

STEP-BY-STEP INSTRUCTIONS

Preparation

Plan for 2 sessions of 1 hour each or 1 session 2 hours long.

- Begin by building personal familiarity with the tools and supplies and by practicing each of the 6 mini-projects in this program.
- Collect the results of your mini-projects together to show patrons at the beginning of the workshop.
- Bring books from your collection or images of hand stitching to pass around. Check in with other librarians on staff who may have book recommendations; you might also do a Google Image search for diagrams of different stitches to print out.
- Create a patron hand-sewing kit for each participant.
- Make a scrap pile that includes some inappropriate fabric scraps.

Program Instructions

Set the stage aloud for the workshop: create a no-judgment, "perfection-is-overrated" zone to free up your patrons and get their creativity flowing. There is beauty in every stitch! However, for mending, the stitches also serve a functional purpose, so stitches must be sized appropriately and secure to make sure that patrons' clothing doesn't fall apart. Collect your mini-projects together to show patrons at the beginning of the workshop. Also bring the books from your collection or images of hand stitching mentioned previously to pass around.

Go over each item in the hand-sewing kit. Show the stitch sampler they are going to make. Acknowledge that there are many ways to do the same thing in sewing. You are demonstrating one way—not the only way. Patrons may want to demonstrate other methods at the end of the session.

Finally, some patrons will naturally stitch faster than others, so if they finish a mini-project quickly, they can practice stitch length and spacing from project no. 1.

How to Thread a Needle and Tie a Knot

- Cut a piece of craft thread as long as your arm. Snip a sharp tip at one end of the thread. *Tip*: Explain that this length of thread is great because it avoids tangling—even though it requires rethreading more often. Untangling long threads takes more time and is frustrating.
- Demonstrate threading the long-eye needle. Demonstrate a second time using a needle threader. Pull the thread through the needle until the 2 lengths are equal.
- Have patrons try threading the needle.
- Once everyone has threaded their needle, demonstrate making a simple knot as shown in diagram 1. The knot should be near the end of the threads.
- Have patrons try tying a knot.
- Patrons now cut, thread, and knot 5 needles. This solidifies the skill and allows the program to move along seamlessly (sew to speak). At the beginning of each session, patrons should prepare at least 5 needles that are threaded and knotted.

Project 1: How to Make the First Stitch and Create a Stitch Grid

- In this project, patrons will learn how to make a stitch, learn about stitch length and spacing, and make a stitch grid.
- Have patrons draw a straight line with the ruler about 4 inches long on the muslin and mark every ¼ inch.
- Demonstrate taking the first stitch starting underneath the muslin, so that the knot won't show. Begin making stitches using the ¼-inch marks.
- Patrons should make their stitches along the marks on the line until they reach the other side.
- Cut the threads to about 4 inches long. Tie the threads into a knot twice. See diagram 2. Trim the excess thread.
- Draw a second line parallel to the first. Patrons should stitch a second line, endeavoring to match the stitch length and spacing of the first line. Knot off.

FIGURE 16.2 | Sewing stitches

Diagram 1: Knot at
end of Threads

Diagram 2: Knot on
Fabric at end of a Line
of Stitching

Diagram 3: Ladder Stitch

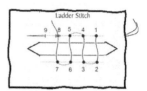

Diagram 4: How to Sew on a Button

Diagram 5: Woven Thread Patch

Diagram 6: Curves, Circles, and Windy Whisps

- Patrons will now create a stitch grid.
- Demonstrate how to turn the fabric 90 degrees and draw 2 new lines perpendicular to the first set. Stitch on these lines to create a grid. Demonstrate how to load several stitches on your needle at one time. *Tip*: Use the geometric terminology—most folks never hear these words used in ordinary conversation.
- Patrons complete the stitch grid. Project no. 1 is now finished. Set it aside. Mention that this is a great stitch for embellishing and is currently very popular. Also mention that chalk can be used to make the lines and then brushed away afterward. And point out that once it has become familiar, stitching can also be done without a line. (At this point, you could also talk about Japanese Sashiko-inspired stitching. Sashiko stitching is an ancient form of mending and extending workwear first practiced by Japanese farmers; see a complete tutorial at https://studio-koekoek.com/how-to-sashiko-stitch-instructions-for-beginners/.)

Project 2: How to Repair or Embellish Items with These Stitch Techniques

- In this project, patrons will mend a tear with invisible stitching using the magical ladder stitch.
- Demonstrate how to sew the ladder stitch, which is basically a straight stitch alternating on each side of a tear. Draw 3 parallel lines about ¼ inch apart (or less) and 1 inch long. Cut the center line (younger tweens may need help with this step). Demonstrate sewing the alternating stitches along each of the remaining lines. Show how the stitches look like a ladder. See diagram 3. Gently pull the stitches to invisibly repair the tear. Magic! *Tip*: Do not pull too tightly or the seam will pucker.
- Have patrons draw their lines, cut a short slit in a piece of muslin, and then sew the ladder stitch.
- Project no. 2 is now completed. Set it aside. Ask patrons to think of potential uses for this stitch. Ideas include closing a seam that pops, closing a hole in a stuffed toy, and so on.

Project 3: How to Sew on a Button

- Knowing how to sew on a button is a valuable skill that patrons can use right away.
- Demonstrate how to mark the placement of the button with a pencil. Mention or show, if possible, that this would be right underneath the buttonhole when a button pops off something.
- Demonstrate bringing the needle into the mark from underneath the fabric and pulling until the knot stops the thread. Slide the button down the thread to the surface of the fabric. Demonstrate stitching into the second hole. Demonstrate bringing the needle back up and peeking under the button to find the hole. Sew 7 or 8 stitches until the button is secure. Explain how to avoid sewing over the edge of the fabric, as this will make the button unusable. Have patrons test each other's buttons to determine when it feels secure enough. Knot off. See diagram 4.
- Have patrons finish sewing their button to another piece of muslin. Project no. 3 is now completed. Set it aside.
- Take a stretch break. Rethread the needles. Thread 1 needle with regular thread.

Project 4: How to Patch Clothing or Accessories

- Demonstrate cutting a small hole in the center of the muslin. To prevent the hole from getting bigger, stitch around the hole with small running stitches using the regular thread.
- Go through the scrap pile—ask patrons whether they think any of the fabrics in the pile would be a poor choice for a patch and if so, why. Show inappropriate fabrics—stretchy, slippery, obviously dry-cleanable, and so on. Mention that the patch fabric and the mended item must be compatible. And mention that stretchy or slippery fabrics can prove difficult to sew for beginners.
- Select a scrap. Cut a small piece of compatible fabric that is at least 1 inch bigger than the hole all the way around.
- Explain the bright side and dull side of a fabric (also called the right side and wrong side). Place the patch over the hole with the bright/right side facing up.
- Demonstrate how to pin the patch to the fabric.

- Demonstrate a raw edge patch. Sew the patch, pointing out that the stitches are at least ¼ inch from the raw edge in order to survive washing. Sew two edges of the patch, with attention to how to turn a corner.
- Demonstrate the folded edge patch on the remaining two edges. Fold under a small amount of the fabric edge and continue sewing stitching near the edge. Sew and fold as you go until the patch is completely sewn. Knot off.
- Have patrons finish sewing the patch in both ways. Project no. 4 is now completed. Set it aside.
- *Tip*: For extra strength, a lightweight piece of fabric can be sewn underneath the patch too. *Tip*: The raw edge patch can be frayed with a pin for a chic look. *Tip*: The patch can also be placed underneath the garment for a modern, visible-mending look.

Project 5: New-Fashioned Darning – How to Make a Woven Thread Patch

- This stitch is a lot of fun. Patrons love it. The cord/floss itself is used to make a patch over a hole.
- Thread patch: Cut a small ½-inch square hole in denim. Make 5 straight parallel stitches about 1 inch long across the square. Knot off underneath the fabric. Pick another needle in a contrasting shade. Bring the needle up near a corner. Weave the needle through the stitches back and forth from one edge to the other. Make a small stitch at the end of each row. Repeat in the opposite direction. Continue until the rectangle is completely filled in. Knot off underneath. A nice woven patch will emerge—more magic! See diagram 5. *Tip*: Weave with the eye-end of the needle to avoid piercing the long stitches.
- Other options: Stabilize the square before stitching; sew a compatible patch underneath the hole before stitching the woven-thread patch; or just embellish your item.
- Project no. 5 is now completed. Set it aside.

FIGURE 16.3 | How to sew a woven patch

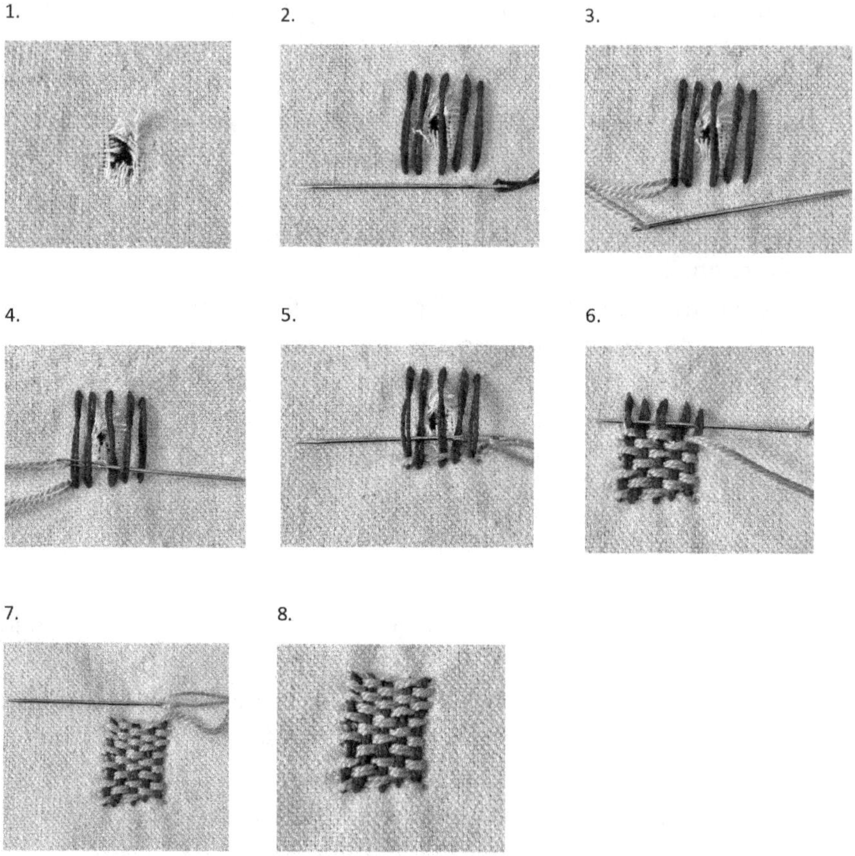

1.

2.

3.

4.

5.

6.

7.

8.

Project 6: Just for Fun—Curves, Circles, and Windy Whisps (an optional project, if there is time remaining)

- Demonstrate drawing a short curvy or spiral line freehand. Stitch along the line with even stitches and knot off at the end. Try stitching parallel curvy lines. Try adjusting the length and spacing to achieve a desired effect. Everywhere that a straight line is used, a curved line can also be sewn. Function is key—simply make sure that the curved line will hold the patch in place. See diagram 6. Patrons can also stitch letters and numbers. This is also the basis for popular stitching in cursive.
- Project no. 6 is now completed. Set it aside.

Finishing Up

- Pass out sturdy envelopes. Each patron will put their work in their individual envelope to take their stitch sampler collection packet home.
- Tidy up: All the leftover supplies should fit in a boot box. Pins and needles should be returned to the pincushions. Take care to check for any pins or needles that may have fallen on the floor. Leftover cord can be wound on paper bobbins.

Sharing

- Discuss ideas for using patches and repair strategies. Bring additional examples in pictures or slides. Refer to the books in your collection. Good ones to have on hand are *Sew It! By Hand* and *Sew It! Tween*, both project-based sewing handbooks by Ellen Lumpkin Brown; *Learn How to Do Hand Sewing Stitches: Plus 20 Projects to Practice Your Skills*, by Sarah J. Doyle; and *Modern Mending: How to Minimize Waste and Maximize Style*, by Erin Lewis Fitzgerald.

RECOMMENDED NEXT PROJECTS

Additional Sessions on Hand Sewing using Ellen's Sew it! Workshop videos (www.sewitworkshop.com/library-program.htm) and optional patron project kits at the library or at home are good ways to keep the momentum going. These videos include topics such as Trendy Mending and Stylish Stitching; Modern Embroidery with the One Straight Stitch Technique; Creating DIY Patches to Repair or/and Adorn (including anime characters!); Minor Fixes and Alterations: Buttons, Hems, Taking in and Letting Out; as well as useful items like the Essentials Mini Bag with Zipper. These Hand Sewing Project Videos are especially designed for libraries and have been enjoyed by thousands of patrons. Sashiko hand stitching programs using any of the popular books is a lovely class. An Introduction to the Sewing Machine workshop is wonderful for libraries that have machines or for patrons to bring their own. Finally, cross-disciplinary programming with other sustainable living initiatives abound—for example, straight stitching is a beautiful way to finish and embellish drying cloths for flowers and herbs.

Melt-and-Pour Glycerin Soap
A Fun Do-It-Yourself Project for Kids and Adults

DANA BRIGANDI

I n this program, participants will learn to create their own homemade glycerin soap using just a few ingredients and the melt-and-pour method. This program is best suited for beginners who are interested in wading into the sudsy field of soapmaking and spa crafts. It also makes a fun holiday program in which participants come away with colored, scented soap they can keep or gift to others. This program works well in small group settings and provides ample opportunities for socialization while the soap is curing.

Age Range	Library Type	Cost Estimate
Tweens (ages 8-12) Young adults (ages 13-18) Adults	Public libraries	$100-$250

FIGURE 17.1
A soapmaking workshop

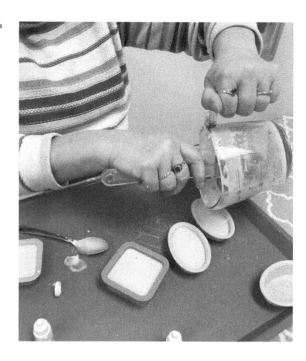

Cost Considerations

Approximately $12 per person, depending on existing supplies

- The base for glycerin melt-and-pour soap can be purchased online or at a local craft store in 2-pound blocks of either clear or white base (typically each block contains 40 scored cubes, with each cube weighing 1.25 ounces). Keep in mind that the colors will vary based on the base color selected. The cost is approximately $15 per 2-pound block.
- Scented oils can be purchased online or at a local craft store (try to match the scents to the color additives or base them on a theme, such as holiday scents or relaxation scents). Typically, only a few drops to a teaspoon of scented oil are needed per participant. You can also ask participants to bring their own favorite essential oil. The total cost is approximately $16 for a set of 6 scented oils.
- Color additive is not necessary but is a fun addition for participants. These can be purchased online or at a local craft store. The cost is approximately $10 for 10 different colors. Make sure the color additive is safe for the skin and is listed for soapmaking.

- Soap molds: Participants can use muffin tins, loaf pans, or silicone baking molds in fun shapes. Silicone molds can be purchased online or at a local craft store. Try to make sure that the molds are shaped like soap, rather than food items, so they will not be mistaken for food.
- Pyrex glass 1-cup or 2-cup measuring cups—one for each participant. You can also ask participants to bring their own cups from home.
- Baking sheets or plastic trays—one for each participant. You can also ask participants to bring their own trays from home or purchase them inexpensively at local thrift shops.

OVERVIEW

This program provides hands-on experience in making glycerin soap using molds, color additives, and scented oils. It is helpful to keep the workshop size small (between 4 and 10 people) to ensure there is adequate space for curing the soap and space for participants to move around. One library staff member can be assisted by a volunteer or second staff member to help participants as needed. Library staff should plan for a 2-hour program with setup, directions, cooling, and cleanup.

NECESSARY EQUIPMENT AND MATERIALS

- Glycerin soap base in blocks (www.amazon.com/Life-Party-Clear -Glycerin-52001/dp/B002PNRVNO) or https://tinyurl.com/ycc3y2de
- Silicone molds (www.amazon.com/TDHDIKE-Silicone-Cavities-Hand made-Cornbread/dp/B087JNT76R) or https://tinyurl.com/2p8pchtw or other baking molds
- Scented oils (www.amazon.com/Favorites-Premium-Grade-Fragrance -Oils/dp/B00C932DU6) or https://tinyurl.com/2p8txfhj
- Color additive (www.amazon.com/Colors-Liquid-Soap-Grade-Gluten -Free/dp/B077WT912J) or https://tinyurl.com/2p92tpmj
- Microwave oven
- Pyrex glass measuring cups (1- or 2-cup size)
- Metal spoons
- Sharp knife
- Baking sheets or plastic trays
- Refrigerator/freezer

- Plastic tablecloths or newspaper
- Plastic gloves
- Safety goggles
- Food scale
- Rubbing alcohol in a spray bottle
- Access to a sink for cleanup

Recommended but Optional Materials

- Small decorative plastic zip-top bags or gift boxes if giving the soap as a gift
- Board games or card games to play while the soap is curing

STEP-BY-STEP INSTRUCTIONS

Preparation

Cover all tables with plastic tablecloths or newspaper. Make sure you have enough supplies so that each program participant can select their own tray, molds, scent, color, and soap base. Create a simple one-sheet flyer about soapmaking and where the supplies were purchased so participants can replicate the project at home if they want. Encourage program participants to wear clothes that can get messy, preferably with long sleeves. Have participants wear gloves and safety goggles while working with the soap base.

Program Instructions

- Use the knife to cut a soap base block into smaller pieces. Weigh the glycerin soap base in a small Pyrex glass measuring cup, dividing it equally among participants. Eight ounces of soap base (approximately four rows of four cubes each) will create approximately three 2 × 2½-inch rectangle-shaped bars.
- Then, heat the glycerin base in a microwave on high, stirring at 30-second intervals, until it is completely melted. This should take approximately 1 to 2 minutes based on the microwave wattage and the size of the soap base cuttings.

FIGURE 17.2 | Glycerin soapmaking supplies

- Add scented oils and color additives as desired and stir to combine.
- Carefully pour the melted soap into the molds. Try not to splash the soap or get too many bubbles. (*Note:* If you do get bubbles in the soap, gently tap the baking sheet or tray on the counter or lightly spray the top of the bar soaps with rubbing alcohol.)
- Place the trays with the molds in the refrigerator or freezer for at least 30 minutes in order to harden (or "cure") the soap.
- Have participants wash their supplies while their soap is cooling.
- Socialize by playing board or card games, or listening to music, while the soap is curing.
- When the allotted time is up, remove the trays from the refrigerator or freezer and gently pop the soap out of the molds.
- If giving the soap as a gift, place them in plastic zip-top bags or small gift boxes.

RECOMMENDED NEXT PROJECTS

Glycerin soap is just one of many soapmaking projects that can be done in a library setting. Try adding other soap bases, such as shea butter, olive oil, castile, oatmeal, goat milk, honey, coconut milk, or aloe, in order to see the differences in color and scent and how the soaps feel on the skin.

Lather Up
Cold-Process Soapmaking for Beginners

ALLISON CICERO MOORE

T his program is a beginner's lesson in creating cold-process soap. Soapmaking has many appealing aspects as a hobby: it is endlessly customizable depending on the available materials, participant needs, and library setting. Furthermore, participants will take home a useful product; and while you can use soap in your own home, it also makes a practical and enjoyable gift.

Soapmaking is much like baking cookies: anyone can do it! Plus, if you pay close attention to a recipe, you'll end up with an excellent and consistent batch. Of course, you'll need to take quite a few more safety precautions than when baking cookies—but I will address those step by step.

This program is designed for 10 participants, and the recipe provided below will create three 3–4 ounce bars of soap per participant.

Age Range	Library Types	Cost Estimate
Older teens (16–18) Adults	Public, school, and academic libraries	$150–$300

Cost Considerations

Many of the items needed for this workshop are up-front, one-time costs. I recommend sourcing as many kitchen tools as possible from secondhand sources to keep costs low. For instance, wire whisks and mixing bowls are an outlay, but they can be washed and reused. (They should not be used for food once used for soap, though.) If you are on a shoestring budget, use only upcycled/recycled molds, and omit fragrance or colorants.

OVERVIEW

First, consider where to hold the workshop. Because you and your participants will be mixing a lye solution, you should plan to do this in a large, open-air space—potentially outside or in an area that opens to outside via a garage door or large windows. *Under no circumstances should you make soap in a small or poorly ventilated room.*

This workshop can be held in 2–3 hours, depending on the skill level of the instructor and if the ingredients are pre-measured. (While it is wonderful for participants to have the experience of weighing their ingredients, it's not necessary for all of them to do this individually—it takes a surprisingly long time.)

Because this workshop requires great care and attention to safety, keep your workshop size small, at 8–10 participants, and have an additional staff member prepared to assist.

The recipe provided below will create three 3–4 ounce bars of coconut oil soap in individual molds. Coconut oil soap hardens quickly, so by the time you're done doing dishes at the end of the workshop, it should be solid enough for participants to take home. If not, participants should be directed to come back the next day (or even the following week).

However: participants *must* wait to use the soap for 24–48 hours to be sure the soap has saponified (for safety), and they *should* wait at least 4 weeks for the soap to cure before use (for quality).

NECESSARY EQUIPMENT AND MATERIALS

- Clothing: Participants should wear long-sleeve shirts, pants, and close-toed shoes.
- Something disposable to protect the table surface—secured cardboard, plastic tablecloth, and so on
- Coconut oil: 1 gallon
- Distilled water: 1 gallon (You must use *distilled*, not "purified," water. Distillation eliminates the possibility of surprise ingredients in your soap.)
- Sodium hydroxide lye: 2 pounds
- Pink salt: about 120 grams
- Nitrile gloves: 2 pairs per participant
- Safety goggles: 1 pair per participant
- Mixing containers
  - 4 large mixing bowls (for oil)
  - 4 medium mixing bowls (for water/lye solution)
  - 4 small bowls or 16-ounce plastic food storage containers (for measuring lye)
  - Note: All mixing containers should be stainless steel, glass, or recycling code 5 (polypropylene) plastic.
  - *Never use items made from aluminum for soapmaking.*

- Infrared thermometer
- Immersion blenders: 2 are recommended
  - Have a backup blender—this is a critical piece of equipment

- Dish detergent (degreaser)
- Molds for soap
  - Many soapers make soap in loaves. That is possible with this recipe at a larger scale, but it is not recommended for this program.
  - You can use upcycled, clean cut-off bottoms of pint or half-pint dairy cartons, potato chip tubes, or even polypropylene plastic food storage containers—anything with a bit of flex for unmolding.
  - Alternatively, you can purchase silicone muffin molds or candy molds.

- Digital scale, measuring grams to 1 decimal point
- Stainless steel whisks: 4

- Silicone heat-proof spatulas: 4+
- Masking tape
- Sharpie
- Bags for take-home

Recommended but Optional Materials

- Colorant: cosmetic clays, micas, or other natural colorants
  - Research colorants via a reputable manufacturer. *Not all colorants are suitable for cold-process soap.*

- Fragrance oil or essential oil
  - Research this via a reputable manufacturer. *Not all oils are suitable for cold-process soap.*

- Measuring spoons for colorants and/or fragrance
- Mini ramekins (1 or 2 ounces) for measuring out small amounts of additives
- Microwave oven or a melting pot with an electric hot plate or portable electric burner
  - If you don't have access to a microwave, you'll need an alternative way to melt your oil. Avoid an open flame for safety reasons.
  - If you are using a hot plate, use a stainless steel saucepan or stockpot to melt your oils. *Do not use aluminum.*

STEP-BY-STEP INSTRUCTIONS

Preparation

The recipe provided below is a single-oil recipe using coconut oil. You can purchase a big tub of coconut oil at any big-box retailer or wholesale outlet. I chose a coconut oil recipe for this program because this oil is easy to melt, it has a long shelf-life, and it makes a soap with big bubbly lather. This recipe also sets up quickly so participants can take the soap home at the end of the workshop. Coconut oil is less practical from a homesteading or sustainability perspective but is useful for learning the process of soapmaking.

However, if you have ready access to rendered lard or tallow, use those—they also make excellent soap. Or, if you are interested in multi-oil recipes for luxury skin care, you can also research those too. *In all cases, calculate your batch size and run your recipe through a lye calculator in order to check the amount of lye you will need to use for your batch size. Never just estimate the approximate amount of lye to use.*

Program Instructions

Before the Program

1. *Review your recipe.* Either before or during the workshop, you will measure out 4 complete sets of this recipe:
   - Distilled water: 308 grams
   - Sodium hydroxide lye: 137 grams
   - Coconut oil: 935 grams
   - Pink salt: 27.5 grams
   - *Optional:* fragrance and colorant based on the manufacturer's recommendations

2. *Prepare your ingredients.* I recommend that you weigh or measure out ingredients for 3 groups of participants ahead of time, and then measure your fourth and final set during the program so your participants can "get the experience."
3. *Are you opting to use fragrance or colorants?* Double-check the appropriate amounts from the manufacturer and weigh these ingredients out, too.
4. *Set your space up.* Secure any table protection—if you have nice worktables, tape down a disposable sheet of plastic on them or cover the tables with newspaper or recycled cardboard. Spilled soap batter will wreck a table quickly.

One Hour Before

1. *Melt the coconut oil.* Within an hour of your program, melt the coconut oil. The oil may re-solidify if you have a very cold ambient temperature, but you can always remelt it if that happens.
2. *Safety first.* Put on your safety gear: long-sleeve shirt, gloves, and goggles or face shield.
3. *Mix your lye solutions—maybe.* If you will be remaining in the classroom and supervising the solutions, you can prepare the solutions ahead

of time and allow them to cool. If you can't supervise them, mix them later. (I'll remind you below.) To mix the lye:

- Make sure your distilled water is in a large enough container to fit it *and* the lye. Your "medium" bowl should be adequate for this. Take a piece of tape and label your bowl: LYE SOLUTION: DO NOT TOUCH.
- Slowly pour the pre-measured lye beads or flakes into the water. Lye *always* goes into the water—never vice versa. (If you pour water over lye, it can "volcano" and sputter, which is very dangerous.)
- Keeping back to not breathe fumes, stir the solution slowly but thoroughly with a silicone spatula to dissolve the lye. The solution will steam and eventually turn clear. Then, carefully move it away from the edge of the table so that it will not be bumped, moved, or knocked over while you prepare other elements of the program.

Getting Class Started

1. *Introduction.* Welcome your participants to class and warn them not to touch any prepared materials on the table. Then, give participants a primer on cold-process soap. Why is it called "cold-process"? Why is it such a big deal? When can they use their soap? Here is a script:

   Cold-process is one of many soapmaking techniques. It is called "cold-process" because no external heat is used to speed saponification (i.e., the chemical process of the mixture becoming soap). Of course, your oils and lye will be warm, but the reaction of the ingredients creates the only heat used to make the ingredients become soap. Hot-process soap is similar, but the emulsified batter is "cooked" in a pot or oven, which speeds the chemical reaction of saponification. This is faster, but it ends up with a stodgier consistency of soap and no time to make all the fun designs you can create with cold-process soap.

   Cold-process is a chemical marvel! Your ingredients do the hard work for you. The downside, though, is that after you make your soap, you'll need to wait 4–6 weeks for it to become truly good soap. During that time water will evaporate out, and the saponification process will complete. Cold-process soap is technically safe to use after 24–48 hours, but it will be crummy soap—it won't lather well, and it might feel harsh on your skin. It also stinks, but just wait. The extra time is so important.

The recipe you'll be using is an all coconut-oil recipe. In the future, you can customize your soap if you decide to continue soapmaking. Further resources are available at the end of this chapter.

In all cases, you must use a lye calculator to verify your recipe—never approximate how much of an ingredient to use. Precision is the key to making safe soap. Speaking of safety . . .

2. *Give participants "the talk."* Safety is the single most important thing you'll share with participants during your program. Stress the importance of wearing their safety goggles and gloves. (Face shields are acceptable, too.) All participants *must* wear long-sleeve shirts, pants, and close-toed shoes. Don't allow any improperly dressed participants to attend your program or even "just watch."

3. *Ahem . . . that wasn't enough about safety.* While lye spills are dangerous, they can be avoided. Direct participants to make sure not to splash any ingredients: move thoughtfully and carefully, and never hurry. Rushing leads to sloppy mistakes. Do not spill beads or flakes of unmixed lye, and don't knock over the lye mixture or freshly mixed soap. If anyone gets lye on their skin, immediately flush the area with running water for at least 15 minutes. If they continue to be concerned or if there is a larger problem, direct the participant to seek professional medical assistance immediately.

4. *Split into groups.* Create groups of 3–4 participants each, and ask them to assemble at the different ingredient stations.

Making Soap

1. *Now that everyone is a little paranoid, mix the lye solutions.* If you didn't mix the lye solutions as directed in the "One Hour Before" section above, do that now. Remember: lye always goes into the water.

2. *Coconut oil.* Is it melted? If it is liquid, proceed to the next step. If it is solid, melt it now.

3. *Temperature checks.* Using your infrared thermometer, check the temperature of your oil and your lye solution. Stir them and test. Ideally, the coconut oil and lye both should be close to 120 degrees Fahrenheit before proceeding.

   • That's hard to time precisely, though. With this recipe, you have some leeway: if both solutions are between 100 and 135 degrees, you can proceed.

   • If the oil and lye solution are both closer to 100 degrees, the soap will take longer to set up, and your participants may need to return the following day to pick up their soap. You may wish to heat the coconut oil to 135 degrees to expedite the process (do not try to heat the lye solution, though).

4. *Mix it up.* Slowly pour the fully dissolved, now-clear lye solution into the melted coconut oil. Slowly mix the two with a whisk first, and then get out an immersion blender.

   • With the blender *fully submerged,* pulse it at low speed for 1 second, wait for it to stop blending, stir around the edges once while off, fully submerge it again, pulse for 1 second, wait for it to stop, stir, and repeat until your mixture reaches "trace."

   • Trace is when the oils and lye solution are fully emulsified but haven't set up fully into soap.

5. *Are we there yet?* Your soap may reach trace quickly—say, after 3 pulses—or it may take a little longer. Go slowly, don't rush! You are aiming for light or medium trace, which is a consistency like vinaigrette salad dressing. Also, if you scoop a bit of the mixture out over the top, it should leave a faint trail.

   • *Don't over-blend.* If you keep blending—like, *a lot*—you'll get a zillion tiny air bubbles in your soap and hit heavy trace. Your batter will rapidly become a semisolid lump of soap (popularly called "soap on a stick").

   • *Uh-oh, it's thick like brownie batter now.* If your soap starts to thicken to brownie batter consistency, pick up your tempo and get it into a mold, pronto. Be careful, but work faster. Skip any additives (colorants, fragrance, salt, etc.) you planned to include and instead prioritize getting what you have into a mold.

6. *Add the pink salt.* At trace, whisk in the salt.
   - Salt is an additive—it changes the properties of the soap slightly, but it is not required.
   - Adding salt in this recipe has two purposes: one is to add a bit of visual interest, and the other is to help the soap bars set up faster. It can be omitted, but then the soap will take longer to set.
   - If using colorant(s), consider omitting the salt. This will allow you more time to work on a design, as the batter will set up more slowly without salt.

7. *Optional:* add colorants and/or fragrance.
   - If you are using colorants or fragrances, add those at light-medium trace.
   - If you are using multiple colorants, you can add scent first, whisk it in, then separate your mixture into different vessels, and add colorants separately.

8. *Pouring the soap.*
   - If you are opting for a simple design, simply pour the soap into your molds at trace. Then, voila: You've made your first soap!
   - If you added colorants, you can experiment with different ways to pour or swirl differently colored batters together. You can use chopsticks to swirl the two, pour batters over one another, or just pour randomly and see what happens.

Cleaning Up

1. *Safety check:* Do you and your participants still have your safety equipment on? You all should. The soap batter is still caustic.
2. *Scrape, scrape, scrape.* Using a rubber spatula, scrape any additional batter into the molds. Be thorough: the more you get out of the containers, the less waste goes down the sink.
3. *Wipe away.* You can also use paper towels to get into areas that are hard to scrape (e.g., an unplugged, disassembled immersion blender). Get as much soap batter off all surfaces as possible so washing up is faster.
4. *Wash away.* With gloves and goggles still on, wash out your containers for reuse. Use degreasing dish detergent and a dedicated sponge.
   - If you are working in a secure/locked space, it is safer to let the soap sit for 24 hours and wash the dishes yourself after the soap

batter has saponified (and is no longer caustic). If that isn't possible, enlist the help of your participants, but again—stress safety! Even diluted soap batter can still give a chemical burn or irritate the skin. Avoid splashes and keep your safety gear on.

5. *Clean your tables.* Throw away any table protection and wipe down the tables. Some soapers like to wipe down their tables using vinegar to neutralize any remaining lye or raw batter; you should research this and see if this is workable or needed in your setting.

Heading Home

1. *Transporting the soap.* The soap your participants just made is still caustic. If possible, it's better for participants to leave their soap bars overnight and pick them up the next day (or even the following week), but that may not be possible.
   - Regardless, the soap should be solid (not fluid or even jiggly) when they transport it.
   - Advise them to keep their soap in the mold for 24–48 hours, then unmold it, and allow it to cure for 4–6 weeks before use. (Curing is as simple as placing the soap on a bathroom shelf for the next 4 weeks.)
2. Provide bags for participants to take their soaps home.
3. Thank participants for attending and provide them with information on further resources.

RECOMMENDED NEXT PROJECTS

The program you just completed is a basic soapmaking endeavor. If you would like to continue down this sudsy path, I encourage you to read books by Anne-Marie Faiola (founder of the *Soap Queen* blog and author of several excellent books, including *Milk Soaps* and *Pure Soapmaking*). *Scientific Soapmaking* by Kevin M. Dunn is a delightfully nerdy resource, with complete information on the chemistry behind cold-process soap.

Once you've learned the basics, you can do a deep dive into designs and colorants—there are endless YouTube tutorials, or you can sign up for more structured lessons through the Handcrafted Soap and Cosmetic Guild, or the Soap Challenge Club. Instagram is also a great inspirational resource.

If you'd like to formulate your own recipes, you can research the different properties of various oils and butters, design your own recipes, and run the recipe through a lye calculator. You can also infuse oils with botanicals from your garden. The possibilities are endless and much like baking: recipes might be similar, but your preferences and passion will always show through. Happy soaping!

PART IV
Homesteading Programs

Library Rooftop Bees and Pollinator Education

DEREK WOLFGRAM

T he Redwood City (CA) Public Library's rooftop beehives have surprised and delighted customers and brought positive media attention to the library. Honey sales by the Friends of the Redwood City Public Library (RCPL) have offset most of the costs of the program, while also creating a unique promotional item to get people excited about the library. The Honey Bee Interpretive Center inside the library and accompanying programs for all ages by a local beekeeper have increased community awareness about pollinators and their importance to the environment. Read on to see how you can create a similar "buzz" around your library.

Age Range	Library Types	Cost Estimate
Kids (ages 3–7) Tweens (ages 8–12) Young adults (ages 13–18) Adults	Public and school libraries	Can be cost-neutral or even slightly profitable

FIGURE 19.1 | Beekeepers Kendal and Garth inspect the RCPL-branded hives on the rooftop of the downtown Redwood City Public Library.

Cost Considerations

In 2021 the RCPL spent about $4,000 on this project while bringing in about $6,000 from honey sales.

OVERVIEW

The central component of this program is to place honeybee hives on a library rooftop or other protected area on your library's property. Unless you happen to have a beekeeper on your library staff, you will probably want to contract with a local beekeeper to manage the hives. The installation and maintenance of the hives requires a minimal time commitment of library staff—the beekeeper will just need a staff liaison who monitors the hives and maintains communication. However, the additional program components will really bring the beehives to the attention of your community and allow you to maximize the benefit of the beehives. Additional program components can include:

- A poster, electronic presentation, or interactive activity center inside the library to help people learn about your bees and pollinators in general.
- Educational programs for kids or adults on pollinators and pollination, planting bee-friendly gardens, beekeeping at home, creating beeswax candles, tasting a variety of honeys, or other bee-related topics.
- Social media to provide community updates and education about the library's bees and bees in general.
- A clear observation hive installed in a safe location for people to view the activity of the bees inside the hive. Alternatively, a camera can provide a live-stream video of the bees' activity inside or outside the hive.
- Sales of "library honey" to help offset the costs of hive maintenance.
- "Bee" creative—your local community may have unique characteristics that can lead to other potential program components or partnerships.

NECESSARY EQUIPMENT AND MATERIALS

- Beehives and bees—many counties have a local beekeepers guild, whose members will likely be enthusiastic about helping you select the exact right equipment and find the best local source for it.
- Supplies to provide a display inside your library about bees and beekeeping:
  - Displays can be as simple as a printed poster.
  - For an electronic display, you will need a monitor or television and a place to mount it in the library. Depending on the content you plan to display, you may need a network connection.
  - An exhibit may include beekeeping tools, as well as interactive activities to teach about bees and how they gather pollen, how they make honey, how bees communicate with each other through a waggle dance, and more.
- If you contract with a beekeeper (highly recommended!) for hive maintenance and honey processing, they will probably have access to all the packaging equipment and jars required.

Recommended but Optional Materials

- For a live-stream video, you will need a video camera such as the outdoor models used for home doorbell/security systems, as well as either an electrical outlet or a solar panel and accessories to keep the camera charged.
- You may want to create a graphic or logo to include on materials about your bees, such as a website or social media, printed wraps for the hive itself, or labels for the honey jars.

STEP-BY-STEP INSTRUCTIONS

Preparation

- Find out whether there are any state or local restrictions on the locations of honeybee hives in your community that would apply to your library property.
- Talk with your library's director, risk manager, and legal counsel about any insurance requirements or other concerns that might arise from keeping bees on your library's property.
- Identify a location where hives can be located without creating direct exposure to major pedestrian paths. Rooftops are ideal for this purpose. Honeybees will generally not sting except when threatened, but there can be large numbers of bees flying around while beekeepers are doing hive maintenance. Coordinate with your landscaping and/or building maintenance staff to ensure that you're not placing hives in an area that will block access to any critical areas or equipment.
- The location of the hives should be easily accessible by your beekeeper, who may need to carry boxes filled with frames of honey weighing 50 pounds or more. Ideally, the beekeeper will not need to walk through a public area of the library to access the hives, as the occasional bee may follow them into the building.
- Develop a contract with your beekeeper, including the costs of hive installation and maintenance, definition of insurance responsibilities, and ownership of the hives. You may also want to build honoraria for your beekeeper for classes and workshops into the same contract if you plan to offer additional programs.

- The contract should also specify how honey from the library hives is distributed. If your library has a limited budget for the program, the beekeeper may be willing to collect and sell your honey themselves in lieu of cash compensation. At the RCPL, we originally split the honey 50/50 with the beekeeper, but once we learned what a desirable commodity library honey was in our community, we decided to keep all the honey and pay the beekeeper a little more. (We recoup the costs by selling the honey, so the bottom line is the same, but we reap the additional benefit of the community enthusiasm for the library honey.)
- If you plan to sell the honey, you may want to work with a nonprofit partner such as a Friends of the Library group. If you plan to sell it yourself, make sure you follow all local regulations related to sales of food products.

RECOMMENDED NEXT PROJECTS

The more programming and activities you offer along with the beehives, the more your community will appreciate your work to create a more sustainable world. Just a few additional examples of complementary programs are:

- Educational exhibits about bees, pollination, or beekeeping
- Informational programs to help community members support pollinators at their own homes
- Seed giveaways to help people plant bee-friendly gardens
- Live-stream videos, social media, or other promotional tools to help people learn about bees
- Partnerships with local elementary or high schools, community colleges, scouting groups, 4H programs, native plant societies, botanical gardens, or other community groups with a focus on education, science, gardening, or agriculture

ADDITIONAL RESOURCES

You can learn more about the RCPL Bees at www.facebook.com/rcplbees or at www.redwoodcity.org/departments/library/rcpl-info/rcpl-s-honey-bees.

How to Start a Food Waste Collection Program

Compost Saves the World—From Garbage to Garden

LYNNE SERPE

Y ou can empower library patrons to take collective action on the issue of food waste by hosting a weekly frozen food waste drop-off program at your library. This program is great for those not ready—or able—to compost at home. The whole family can get involved, from collecting and freezing their food waste at home, to dropping off the frozen scraps in collection bins set up just outside the library.

Food waste collection programs divert organic waste from the landfill, reducing methane emissions. If you don't have a compost system on-site, you can partner with a local community garden or farm to turn food scraps into nutrient-rich compost, turning trash into treasure and keeping local resources in the local community.

Age Range	Library Types	Cost Estimate
Kids (ages 3–7)	Public and	$50–$100
Tweens (ages 8–12)	school libraries	
Young adults (ages 13–18)		
Adults		

FIGURE 20.1 | James Brinson drops off food scraps at the library.

Cost Considerations

The primary cost for this program is the bins that you will collect frozen food scraps in. If your program becomes popular over time, you may need to increase either the size or the number of collection bins.

OVERVIEW

Community food waste collection programs can divert thousands of pounds of food waste from the landfill each month. The average U.S. household throws away nearly a third of their purchased food, with an estimated aggregate value of $240 billion annually.

Food waste collection programs can last for as long as you would like, but they should be offered on a regular schedule, such as once a week. Longer collection hours are more convenient for participants, but 90 minutes is a good length if you would like to have someone hosting the collection the entire time. It will take no more than 15 minutes for setup and 15 minutes for closing, bringing the total staff (or volunteer) time to 2 hours.

Only one staff person or volunteer is needed to bring out the collection bins from where they are stored and put up any informational signage. During the collection itself, it is good to have someone track the number of participants, make sure no contaminated items are thrown in the bins, and answer any questions.

The only limit on participation is based on the size and number of collection bins you're able to store and put out during the collection, and the capacity of your garden/farm partner or the compost system at your library. The average household brings approximately 4–8 pounds of food scraps each week, depending on household size and the kinds of food they eat.

NECESSARY EQUIPMENT AND MATERIALS

- 20-gallon containers with lids can be used to collect frozen food scraps
- 32-gallon toters with wheels can weigh 100–125 pounds when full
- Informational signage
- A garbage receptacle for any plastic waste or other unacceptable items
- A place to compost the scraps—either a compost system at your library site or a partner garden/farm that will take the scraps away to be composted
- If you compost on-site, you will also need to obtain "browns" such as leaves, mulch, straw, or shredded cardboard. These are your carbon source. Food scraps are mostly your nitrogen source—also known as "greens." Some locations may allow program participants to drop off bags of leaves, space permitting.

Recommended but Optional Materials

If you choose to have a compost bin on-site, there are many options. Cost, space, and the staff's ability to maintain it are important aspects to consider. Enclosed systems, like a tumbler or other durable backyard compost bin, will help avoid smells and avoid attracting rodents but have a much smaller capacity. A three-bin system will take up more space but have greater capacity. Any of these options can be made from recycled or repurposed materials or purchased new.

STEP-BY-STEP INSTRUCTIONS

A weekly food waste collection program can be very simple to run as long as you have a reliable garden/farm partner or the ability to compost on-site. The amount of food scraps collected will depend on the popularity of your program over time, but you should expect to collect hundreds of pounds a week.

Preparation

- If you are not composting scraps on-site, you will need a partner garden or farm where scraps can be taken and composted.
- Your partner garden/farm should collect the scraps within 24–48 hours of the collection, before the frozen scraps have thawed out entirely.
- You need to have a place to store the collection bins when empty. (If this is an outdoor space, you may also wish to lock them up.)
- You need to have an outdoor space to store the full bins.
- Full bins should be easily accessible by your garden/farm partner so they can pick up full bins each week, and leave empty, rinsed bins behind.
- You need a way to rinse the bins (if your farm/garden partner is unable to do so).
- You need an outdoor space with protection from the rain to host the collection program.

Program Instructions

Setting up for the program is as simple as bringing out the empty collection bins from where they are stored to an outdoor area that is convenient for participants to access. You may also choose to post informational signage.

At the end of the program, full and empty bins can be brought back to the appropriate storage location outside, to be picked up by your garden/ farm partner within 24–48 hours or taken to your compost area on-site to be processed.

During the program, staff or volunteers are mostly there to track participation and ensure that no contaminated scraps are thrown into the bins. They may be asked a number of questions from participants or observers, such as:

Why do food scraps need to be frozen?

- Freezing the scraps avoids potential smells during the collection itself.
- Freezing the scraps means no smells, fruit flies, roaches, or rodents for participants at home.
- Freezing the scraps breaks down the cell membranes of plant matter, speeding up the decomposition process.

What kind of container should participants use to freeze their scraps?

- Encourage reuse! Participants can use whatever container will fit in their freezer, such as yogurt containers, loose-leaf salad containers, Tupperware containers, or even Ziploc bags.
- Brown paper bags can be emptied of their contents and then torn up and placed in the bins.
- Compostable bags can be emptied of contents and then placed in the bins.
- Plastic bags or non-reusable containers should be put in the garbage if they cannot be rinsed and recycled by participants at home.

What items are acceptable for the food waste collection program?

- Fruit and vegetable scraps (peels, pits, seeds)
- Eggshells, nut shells, seed shells
- Tea bags, coffee grounds, filters
- Plain grains, plain pasta, or plain bread

What items are NOT acceptable for the food waste collection program?

This will depend on your garden/farm partner, but typically:

- No meat, no bones, no dairy, no oily foods
- Participants should remove stickers and, if possible, any staples from tea bags
- No pet waste or human waste
- No yard waste (unless you have the capacity to accept bags of leaves)
- No human or pet hair or dryer lint (unless your garden/farm partner allows)

Are compostable bags, plates, cups, forks, etc., acceptable?

This will depend on your garden/farm partner. Many "compostable" items will only compost in a municipal facility or in larger composting systems. Other items have been imprinted with PFAS (per- and poly-fluoroalkyl substances), which your partner may wish to exclude.

- Limiting the collection to food scraps only is the simplest method.
- As some participants will choose to freeze their scraps in compostable bags, they can be allowed to place those bags in the bins if your garden/farm partner is able to process them.

RECOMMENDED NEXT PROJECTS

Once your food waste collection program is up and running, you can think about ways to encourage library patrons to compost at home—thus reducing food waste even more and enabling them to use the compost produced in their own gardens.

If your library has an outdoor space where you can have (and maintain) a demonstration compost bin, this would enable you to offer hands-on experiential composting workshops. You can also host programs about building an easy compost bin out of a regular trash can, wooden pallets, or cinder blocks.

An indoor option is "vermicomposting," where red wiggler worms do the work for you. Worm bins are very easy to make from a 10-gallon container with lid, a drill to make air holes, and a starter batch of red wiggler worms that are available online.

If you have a staff kitchen area, you could keep your indoor worm bin and hold a weekly program where you have children help feed the worms, either from scraps collected in your staff kitchen or taken from collection bins. Red wiggler worms like temperatures from 50 to 80 degrees, so any scraps fed to the worms should be thawed out first.

Other great program options for food planning and preparation include the efficient use of leftovers and programs about pickling, canning, and preserving. Reducing the amount of surplus food waste each household produces is the top tier of the food waste recovery hierarchy.

Composting at Home

CATHERINE JOHNSON and MAGGIE PINNICK ANDREJKO

C omposting is a way to recycle organic matter, like food scraps and grass clippings, into a nutrient-rich fertilizer. The best part is that it's great for the environment too. A composting program is a great homesteading topic to offer because it is an accessible program for many patrons. Composting can be done in homes with big backyards, as well as school yards or college campuses.

In this program patrons will learn the basics of composting through a guided discussion. This can be content-heavy, so it's great if community partners and other local people who already compost are there to share their real-world experiences.

Age Range	Library Types	Cost Estimate
Adults	Public and academic libraries	$0–$50

OVERVIEW

This composting program offers an introduction to composting principles. It can be as simple as a PowerPoint presentation followed by a discussion of composting knowledge and experiences among patrons, or an in-depth presentation with opportunities to see active composting and interact with compost. This program topic lends itself well to inviting local practitioners to be a part of the conversation and to share their knowledge. Some university extension groups have Master Composters as part of their Master Gardeners program. These people are great resources for composting conversations and may be able to bring compost samples or equipment.

NECESSARY EQUIPMENT AND MATERIALS

- Computer and projector for PowerPoint or similar presentation
- A room with chairs for attendees

Recommended but Optional Materials

- Compost thermometer (borrow or purchase)
- One or more samples of actual compost—ideally, several samples in different stages of breaking down—in clear glass jars that can be passed around
- One or more compost bins for display—either in the presentation room or outside on the premises
- Ingredients for "compost cupcakes" (recipe included in slide materials), plates, and/or napkins
- Copies of an EPA composting handout: https://nepis.epa.gov/Exe/ZyPDF.cgi/P1006PSV.PDF?Dockey=P1006PSV.PDF (or https://tinyurl.com/3v2rc6a9) or a similar handout from the local university extension

STEP-BY-STEP INSTRUCTIONS

Preparation

A fun option may be to bake a batch of compost cupcakes for the group using the recipe provided below to serve at the end of your presentation.

You can research composting basics if needed (https://www.epa.gov/recycle/composting-home) and obtain data about the amount of compostable material in the local waste system.

Create a PowerPoint or similar presentation with basic information about composting. Slide content may include:

- An optional opening slide with local data about the amount of compostable material in the local waste system.
- A slide defining composting as:
  - Decomposition of organic matter
  - Ideal ratio of carbon to nitrogen: 25 to 1 (by weight, not volume)
  - The meaning of "brown" and "green" in composting. "Brown" denotes carbon-rich leaves and mulch, while "green" denotes nitrogen-rich food scraps. In a similar vein, "brown" denotes dry materials (dead leaves), while "green" denotes fresh and moist materials (food scraps).
  - 1 bucket, packed: 2 buckets (Another way of thinking of this ratio is in terms of the brown and green composting buckets. For every 1 brown bucket (packed), it would have 2 buckets of green compost material.)
  - Composting requires water, oxygen, and microbes.
  - Talking points: The microorganisms that decompose organic matter use carbon as a source of energy and nitrogen for building their cell structure. They need more carbon than nitrogen. But if there is too much carbon, decomposition slows when the nitrogen is used up and some of the microorganisms die. Too much carbon thus slows down decomposition. However, too much nitrogen releases ammonia and creates a stinky pile. The microorganisms need water and oxygen—stir the pile somehow to allow water to soak through to its lower layers. The final humus that is formed is 50 percent carbon and 5 percent nitrogen, or a ratio of 10 to 1.
- A slide illustrating common sources of carbon and nitrogen. A website that has a great infographic is www.fix.com/blog/how-to-start-a-compost-pile/.
- Talking points: Dried leaves are key and are plentiful in the fall; in the summer, grass clippings can really heat up a compost pile.

- Provide a slide about ideal temperatures in a compost pile. The optimum temperature range is 135 degrees to 160 degrees Fahrenheit. You can obtain a graph from http://whatcom.wsu.edu/ag/compost/fundamentals/needs_carbon_nitrogen.htm.
- Talking points: High temperatures are essential for the destruction of pathogenic organisms and undesirable weed seeds in the pile. Also, decomposition is more rapid in the thermophilic temperature range of 135 degrees to 160 degrees. At this point in the presentation, librarians can show and pass around the compost thermometer.
- Other slides may include:
  - A slide with a picture of various compost bins—do a Google Image search or take pictures of bins you have seen.
  - A slide with recommendations on typical uses for compost, such as spreading it on garden beds in the fall, planting in it in the spring, or using it as a top dressing for seeded vegetables and flowers.
  - Talking points: Signs that a compost pile may not be ready include the following ones:
    - Recognizable food content is still visible.
    - The pile is still warm. This means that it is still working.
    - There are still lots of large lumps in the pile.
- An optional slide could include a "compost tea" recipe—use the step-by-step instructions for this at www.groworganic.com/blogs/articles/compost-tea-how-to-make-one-version-of-it.
- Talking points: With compost, one can add worm castings and/or a catalyst like unsulphered molasses (½ ounce per gallon). Worm castings, a fancy name for worm poop, contain active microbes and dissolve easily in water. Molasses feeds the beneficial microbes in the soil. Other optional supplements include liquid kelp (a source of minerals) and liquid fish (emulsion). Fish emulsion is a source of nitrogen, which is good for young plants at the growth stage. Bat guano can also be added as it provides phosphorus to improve flowers and fruit.
- Compost tea can be sprayed on a plant's leaves (referred to as a foliar spray) to feed leaf microbes. This can actually protect the leaves, as active microbes improve the plant's immune system. *Clean* all equipment thoroughly afterward by rinsing with warm water. Do *not* use antimicrobial soap as it may inhibit microbial activity in future batches on compost tea. A natural soap could be used if necessary.

- An optional slide that shows the advantages of composting:
  - It enriches the soil and helps it to retain moisture.
  - It reduces the need for chemical fertilizers.
  - It reduces methane emissions from landfills.

- You could also provide an optional slide with the recipe for making "compost cupcakes":
  - Use any basic chocolate cupcake recipe or box mix and add in shredded carrot, oats, crushed potato chips, and a pinch of coffee grounds (decaf).
  - Top with chocolate frosting (homemade or store-bought).
  - Dip each cupcake in "dirt" (crushed graham crackers and/or chocolate animal crackers) and "grass clippings" (shredded coconut dyed green).
  - Decorate with a gummy worm.
  - *Optional:* Use a gluten-free cupcake mix and gluten-free cracker crumbs.

Program Instructions

- On the day of the program, set up the room in advance by arranging chairs so that patrons will be able to see the presentation easily. If you have compost bins or jars of compost to display, set them out so that they are easily visible as patrons enter and exit or are set on tables at the front of the room where they will be easily seen.
- Have plates and/or napkins available if you will be serving compost cupcakes.
- Ask participants what experience they have had with composting.
- Ask participants to guess what percentage of trash in U.S. landfills is actually compostable:
  - The answer, taken from the EPA's 2018 graph on municipal solid waste (trash), is approximately 33 percent (food waste + yard trimmings).

- Give the slide presentation.
- Facilitate a Q&A time, allowing experienced composters to share their knowledge.
- Invite people to enjoy a cupcake.

- Have participants feel (when appropriate), smell, and describe the compost after the presentation.
- Have books on composting, gardening, and recycling displayed. Leave composting instructions and guides for patrons to take home and continue their learning.

RECOMMENDED NEXT PROJECTS

Vermiculture (composting with worms) is a possible next topic because it is an indoor composting method that can be accommodated to apartment living. A good vermiculture resource is www.epa.gov/recycle/how-create-and-maintain-indoor-worm-composting-bin.

Another possible follow-up program would be to host a "Build Your Own Compost Bin" workshop. Bins can be built out of wood pallets and chicken wire. County conservation district managers and university extension office agents can be great partners for this. See www.thespruce.com/compost-bin-plans-4769337.

How to Prepare for Raising Chickens
Basic Facts to Raise Chicks and Chickens

ANGELA HOGG

I f you've ever wondered how to begin raising chickens to benefit from their delicious fresh eggs, then you've come to the right place. The first thing to know is that it isn't hard, and the simple facts you need to know to get started can be found right here. In learning about baby chicks and laying chickens, you will understand how to meet their basic needs and also discover the joy that chickens can bring. This chapter will help librarians teach patrons how to prepare for raising their own flock of chickens.

AGE RANGE

This project is geared to the unsupervised, independent caretaking of chickens, but with supervision younger age groups could participate as well.

- Ages 8 to adult unsupervised
- Ages 3–7 supervised

FIGURE 22.1 | Baby chicks starting out in a brooder

Library Types	Cost Estimate
Public and school libraries	$150–$3,000

Cost Considerations

If you have materials lying around with which to put together a small house for a few birds in a flock, or you find a chicken coop for free that someone has finished using, then you could easily start on the lower end of the cost scale. Coops can be as fancy as you want them to be and can easily cost $3,000 or even more, depending on the size of the flock and the rarity of the breed of chickens you choose.

OVERVIEW

Overall, raising chickens is not a difficult task, but the fact that there are often no clear guidelines as to how to prepare can make the whole process a little intimidating. For example, there are many different varieties and sizes of chickens. There are standard-sized varieties such as Orpingtons,

Rhode Island Red, Isa Brown, and Marans. Then there are skinnier, less meaty breeds such as Ameracaunas, Ayam Cemani, and Schijndelaar. The smallest sizes are called bantams, which include mostly silkies, but other breeds can be bred to the smaller bantam size too. If you are interested in larger chickens, there are a few breeds that grow as tall as 2–3 feet, such as Jersey Giants, Liege Fighters, and Ayam Ketawa. The types of birds you choose also helps determine the size coop you need, along with the types of feed and watering supplies. There are also many different ways that you can design a chicken house (coop). When it comes down to it chickens need food, water, and shelter just like any other animal, so keep that in mind. This chapter will break down chicken raising from start to finish so that you can instruct patrons as to how they can enjoy raising them and eating their delicious eggs.

Considerations include where you want to start (baby chicks or older chickens), what is needed for a healthy setup for them to live in, and information on how to keep them happy so they will produce eggs. Librarians can choose to construct a small coop and keep chickens for their programming, or they can create instructional workshops designed to teach patrons how to get set up themselves.

NECESSARY EQUIPMENT AND MATERIALS

- Heat source (if starting with baby chicks)
- Enclosed smaller area for baby chicks, or a henhouse for larger, older birds
- Water provider
- Food provider
- Chicken coop (size depends on how many birds in your flock)
- Bedding, preferably pine shavings

Recommended but Optional Materials

- Mealworms
- Fresh greens (no tomato plants, but the birds can have actual tomatoes)
- Chicken scratch (a mix of corn and seeds)
- Extra roost areas for them to climb high and sit
- Diatomaceous earth for dust bathing

STEP-BY-STEP INSTRUCTIONS

Preparation

Before starting on the journey of raising chickens, a person must decide to begin with either chicks, pullets (adolescent hens), or mature hens. The benefit to starting with chicks is having the opportunity for them to know you from the start and begin a relationship with you. If you would like chickens to eat out of your hand, then starting with chicks would increase the possibility of this happening. Pullets, adolescent hens, are still young enough to establish this type of trusting relationship as well, but they have already started to become more independent. A fully mature laying hen will take much longer to trust you but will eventually learn a schedule and a routine.

Where to Get Baby Chicks

Choosing to start with chicks brings up the question, "where do I get baby chicks?" There are a few ways to obtain them. First, there are the farm supply stores such as Tractor Supply and Rural King, and even your local feed and grain store might possibly stock baby chicks each spring. These chicks are hatched from different farms or breeders and are sent to the stores in masses. You must keep in mind that these chicks have been exposed to different environments, and sometimes have been handled by different people, ranging from workers in the stores to customers. Being aware of this is important because all these factors can contribute to possible sickness that the chicks can bring to your flock—though this is by no means a certainty. Many chicks are bought every year from local farm supply stores without having any problems.

Another way to purchase chicks is from the website of a hatchery or farm—sites, for example, like www.cacklehatchery.com or www.meyer hatchery.com/index.html. Typically these chicks are more expensive because they have received more detailed care and the quality of the breeding stock is higher, which in turn produces prettier and sometimes healthier birds. You can also find rare and exotic breeds of chickens from private farms. If you choose to buy from a local farm privately, sometimes you will be able to tour the farm and see how the chicks are taken care of; and if a problem subsequently develops with your chicks, then often the breeder will work with you, unlike the farm supply stores. Local farms can often be found on Facebook through groups or through the postings on bulletin boards at a local farm or feed store.

Program Instructions

Starting with Baby Chicks

Once you decide where you will obtain your chicks, the next step is having an area ready for them to live and grow. This area needs to have heat, food, and water. The heat can be sourced from a heat lamp or a heat plate. Heat lamps are the easiest and cheapest way to provide heat, but they can be the most dangerous way as well. Many fires have been caused by heat lamps when users weren't careful to mount them properly. Heat plates cost more, but they have a lesser danger factor. Chicks need to have access to heat for up to at least 4 weeks after hatching. This gives them the time needed to grow their actual feathers for warmth. Examples of a good starting "brooder" would be an extra large Rubbermaid container, or a simple 4-foot-tall box built out of plywood and metal hardware, with a cloth awning on top. We have used both of these types to get our chicks started. An old dresser or chest could also be used if the shelves are taken out. The chicks need enough space to be able to go near the heat source when they want to and also be able to escape the heat when they feel too hot.

Food and water are the other two things required for the chicks. When choosing the food for baby chicks, you want to make sure to have "chick starter/grower" crumbles. These can also be purchased with medication included in the feed. You don't have to have the feed medicated, though. In fact, if you're buying chicks from a private breeder, unless that breeder was using medicated feed, then it is recommended to not use it. However, if you're buying chicks from a farm supply store, it is recommended to use medicated feed in order to help ward off sickness due to any contamination. This is not a decision to fret over, however, because as long as the chicks have a clean and heated environment with plenty of food and water, they will be just fine most of the time.

Chicks eat just as much food as a grown hen, so their food container needs to be filled continuously. Moreover, because they are being housed in a smaller area, there is a lot of waste to dispose of. It is very important to keep their living area as clean as possible.

What If I Choose Pullets to Start With?

Pullets are the adolescent stage of hens. This is the stage where it is obvious that the chick is in fact a hen but is not old enough to lay an egg. Pullets can typically be identified once a chick is at least 12 weeks old, but even then, with some breeds it can be very difficult to tell the difference between the sexes at that age. In any case, a pullet can be allowed access to the outside at this point, so this is an advantage of starting with pullets. Pullets typically cost more than chicks but less than a laying hen. They can be put immediately in a coop with access to the outside without worrying about providing heat. Once a pullet reaches 18 weeks, then you can also switch the feed to "layer pellet or crumble." Some birds can be picky about these and will eat one brand better than another. This is the stage of food that chickens remain on.

Laying Hens

Skipping the younger months of a hen's life can save time and trouble. A laying hen is the easiest to begin with by far. This means that eggs should be or are already coming for you to reap the rewards! Laying hens are also fully feathered, so weather elements won't be a factor. Laying hens typically cost the most, especially depending upon the breed. The more exotic or rare the breed, the higher the price (same as chicks). Laying hens of more rare breeds are also more difficult to locate.

Uh-oh. My Pullet Is Actually a Rooster?

This happens more often than not, unfortunately. If you began with chicks from the store, or from a website, then you (sadly) can be stuck with that rooster to do with as you choose. If you purchased chicks or pullets from a private local breeder, sometimes you can work with them on an arrangement about any roosters in the flock. Don't fret too much though; having a rooster also has its benefits. A rooster provides natural protection of your hens. He will work hard to keep predators away and will warn the flock of any potential danger. Having a rooster in your flock will not affect your eggs, unless you have a broody hen. Then you can choose to allow her to continue to sit on the eggs and let nature take its course, or you can collect the eggs daily just like normal.

Housing for a Flock

Chicken coops can come in all shapes and sizes. They can be fancy or as easy as a wooden box. An actual chicken coop needs to provide protection from the weather elements and provide a dry environment, typically one off the ground. We have built several coops simply by printing off instructions or designs from Pinterest and other Google sites. There are also books on how to construct coops, such as *Hentopia* by Frank Hyman (www.storey. com/books/hentopia), which is filled with projects on how to build many different types of chicken shelters. If you are looking to buy an easy kit or a coop that is already built, then Tractor Supply, My Pet Chicken, and Amazon are all good places to start; they have many sizes and designs to choose from, and they will spare you the time and effort spent building a coop from scratch.

The size of the coop depends on the size of your flock. A good rule to go by is 3 square feet per bird. The coop can have a fenced-in area surrounding it, thus providing extra protection from predators and keeping the flock together; or if you would like the chickens to free range, that is completely up to you. Inside the coop you need one nesting box area per three birds.

FIGURE 22.2 | A typical chicken coop

They do share this space. Then, of course, you need a food and water area, and it is best to have these up off the floor of the coop as well. This makes it easier for the birds to eat from, as well as helping to keep the food and water clean. There are many devices to choose from in stores and on the internet for the food and water. Please remember that you are the only one who can choose what is best for you, and this might mean trying a few different ones. Inside the coop you will also want a type of bedding. Do *not* use cedar or Styrofoam in your coop. Chickens peck, and pecking either of these materials will lead to death for your flock. The most common options for inside coops are pine shavings or horse pellet bedding. These provide dust for the birds to roll around in and clean themselves, along with warmth. Both pine shavings and pellet bedding will need to be shoveled once a week and replaced with fresh bedding. Again, you want to keep the birds' home area as clean as possible. Another option is to use sand, but sand creates more weight for coops up off the ground, and this is not ideal. Sand is more commonly used in fenced areas in order to lessen the mud. Sand can be shoveled or "turned over" like tilling a garden to help keep the area fresh. Dirty sand can also be scooped up, like kitty litter.

Keeping chickens is definitely something to enjoy. Once someone gets used to fresh eggs from birds that are able to eat fresh grass and insects, buying store-bought eggs typically becomes less attractive. Chickens are hearty animals, but they can always be replaced easily as well. Whether you start with chicks, pullets, or laying hens, there are enjoyment and rewards at each stage, with finding your first laid egg as the real treasure.

Life after Establishing a Coop

Once you have your flock set up in their own coop and ranging area, some thought should be given to keeping them safe. Chickens are easy prey for predators such as hawks, foxes, coyotes, and even snakes. Hawks are probably the easiest predators to protect from because enclosed fencing or aerial netting draped over the area will provide excellent protection from them. The ground predators create more work for chicken owners. Roosters will help provide some protection, so even though they aren't loved as much, they are great at warning their hens to take cover, and they are known for fighting off hawks, snakes, mice, and rats. If you're capable of having outside guard dogs, they can be extremely helpful if they're accustomed to the birds. And finally, there is the option of digging and anchoring your fencing in the ground, or even placing concrete bricks around the fence's perimeter. After all, you've made it this far with your flock, and these birds cannot protect themselves.

Birds Like to Have Fun Too

Chickens truly do enjoy playing and sunbathing! Yes, you read that correctly, chickens love to roost up high. They are happy to flutter up onto low tree branches or perches that you can create from sticks or any type of wood. Some chickens even like to swing. If you find a toy metal xylophone, you may even hear them making music one day and pecking out some tunes. Along with playing, snacks are also welcomed. Chickens love fresh worms or even dried ones. Chicken scratch, which consists of corn and various seeds, is a nice treat (but not too much). This is like candy to them. If you're growing a garden, any fresh vegetables will quickly be eaten up when thrown into the coop area. The healthier the chickens eat, the healthier you will be too, by reaping the reward of their eggs.

Always remember that there is no one specific way to create a flock of chickens, and another good thing to remember is that chickens can easily be replaced. With the steps described in this chapter, library patrons should be able to easily get started with their own flock to enjoy.

RECOMMENDED NEXT PROJECTS

After you've completed this project, you may follow up with a program on chicken maintenance, an ongoing chicken farmers' club at the library, or similar programming.

All about Chickens
A Hands-on Workshop

JENNIFER MURTOFF

K ids will learn about chickens, eggs, and feathers in this hands-on presentation. After a brief general lesson, children will examine topics on their own at different stations. You can also give them the opportunity to interact with a live chicken!

Age Range	Library Types	Cost Estimate
Kids (ages 3–7) Tweens (ages 8–12)	Public and school libraries	$0–$50

OVERVIEW

This interactive program allows young participants to learn about chickens: their physical characteristics, eggs, and feathers. If available and the facility allows, you might consider bringing a live chicken and allowing kids to interact with it.

The instructor will provide some basic background information on chickens in a short talk prior to sending the kids to the stations. In the talk, kids will look at pictures that show the diversity of chickens: they come in different sizes, colors, and shapes. They will learn some basic differences between male and female chickens, as well as general anatomy. Next, the instructor will discuss the different kinds of feathers found on a chicken's body. Finally, the instructor will show kids the parts of an egg. If there is time, you can show a picture of a developing embryo inside an egg. Allow about 15 minutes for this presentation.

Once the talk is done, the instructor will break the kids into groups. Each group will go to 1 of 3 (or 4) stations. Place 4–5 kids at each station. You should also have an adult (a total of 3–4) at each station to supervise the activity and guide the kids' participation. Instructions for each station will be provided. The stations are as follows: (1) images of chickens, (2) exploring feathers, (3) looking at eggs (whole, raw), and (4) meeting a chicken (optional). The live chicken station may require 2 adults. Program capacity depends on the number of stations you have. Set a maximum of 15 participants if you have 3 stations, and 20 participants if you have 4 stations. Once kids have spent about 10 minutes at a station, they can move on to the next one until they have completed all the stations.

NECESSARY EQUIPMENT AND MATERIALS

For the Talk

- The PowerPoint presentation for this program is available at https://drive.google.com/file/d/1poNwFpjFzljDzkR8mOWK4EO4b-fVOpxv/view?usp=sharing or at https://tinyurl.com/5n75y2um.

Station 1 (Crazy Chickens)

- The photos of chickens (from calendars, books, online) should show different shapes, sizes, and colors of the birds; different breeds, such as silkies, frizzles, Polish, feather-footed breeds, bantams, and large fowl; and different combs, feather patterns, leg colors, body shapes, and skin colors. Include an image of a hen and a rooster of the same breed to highlight the differences between the sexes.

- Crazy Chickens lessons are available at https://drive.google.com/file/d/1Gz90LiGxFCJwwTOqnkuv83m66bBZtV3Z/view?usp=sharing or at https://tinyurl.com/mpk96fum.
- The Crazy Chickens worksheet, with wordbank, is available at https://drive.google.com/file/d/1R9yWyeSbfrVzBtUrIlYEencTydyXFWw-/view?usp=sharing, or without wordbank, at https://drive.google.com/file/d/1fzZl1GPLFS4_6F-MHQTmYHpzmEawmR_k/view?usp=sharing or https://tinyurl.com/2p8bv4y3.
- Paper
- Crayons, colored pencils

Station 2 (Fantastic Feathers)

- Show kids the various types of chicken feathers: down, flight, and contour. The feathers should be labeled, perhaps in plastic bags or on a paper plate.
- The Fantastic Feathers lesson is available at https://drive.google.com/file/d/1oUol6pbBSGijpTCgSzHihfUJ6A89PS_9/view?usp=sharing or at https://tinyurl.com/2p83yhd8.
- The Fantastic Feathers worksheet is available at https://drive.google.com/file/d/14AjcTpFvc6LL1hK8OAMlvNOFlkNN6LIv/view?usp=sharing or at https://tinyurl.com/2z8xdy3s.
- Paper
- Crayons, colored pencils

Station 3 (Incredible Eggs)

- Show kids a fresh egg, broken into a clear glass dish on a dark surface so they can see its various components. The yolk should be intact.
- The Incredible Eggs lesson is available at https://drive.google.com/file/d/1JZ-e1lLyruK0dXXaPuf8_hy9MgGlb_Jd/view?usp=sharing or at https://tinyurl.com/e4c46kn5.
- Photos (or a carton) of eggs of different colors, shapes, and sizes
- Paper
- Crayons, colored pencils

Recommended but Optional Materials

Station 4 (Meet a Chicken)

- A chicken
- Paper towels
- Hand sanitizer

STEP-BY-STEP INSTRUCTIONS

Preparation

Download the PowerPoint presentation, the lessons for the stations, and the worksheets.

Setup: The classroom setup faces a screen for a short presentation to start the class. Stations are set up around the room. Place materials at each station. You may want to provide a handout for the adults at each station that includes the information the kids will be learning.

Program Instructions

Slide Presentation

The following is recommended content for use with the PowerPoint presentation.

- All about chickens! (slide 1): Welcome kids and tell them they are going to learn all about chickens today.
- What do you know about chickens? (slide 2): Begin by asking kids what they know about chickens. Accept all reasonable responses. Prompt responses by asking questions:
  - What kind of animal are chickens? (bird)
  - How are they different from animals like cats and dogs? (feathers, scales on legs, beak, etc.)
  - What do chickens eat? (insects, worms, grass, grains like wheat and corn, fruit, veggies, meat, and small animals—chickens are omnivores)
  - Where do baby chickens come from? (eggs)
  - What colors are chickens? (white, brown, black, tan, patterns)
  - What colors are their eggs? (white, brown, blue, green)

- What is a boy/girl chicken called? (rooster/hen)
- How are chickens like lizards? (they have scales and lay eggs)

■ Colors, shapes, sizes (slide 3): Show kids the pictures of chickens. Guide kids to notice and indicate the different colors of feathers, body shapes, colors of legs and skin (e.g., a silkie has purple skin). Look at the ornamental feathers: muffs (feathers on cheeks), beards (feathers under beak), feathered legs/feet, and crests (feathers on head). Then look at differences in combs (size and kinds).

■ Parts of a chicken (slide 4): Ask about and name some of the body parts (eye, beak, tail, legs, feet, claws, comb on top of head, wattles under beak, feet with claws, wings, earlobe under tuft of feathers behind eye, ear under tuft of feathers behind eye, etc.).

■ Hen and rooster (slide 5): Tell kids that the male is the rooster, the female is the hen. First ask how they are the same (comb, wattle, legs, toes, eyes, earlobes, etc.). Then ask them to point out the differences between them. The rooster is bigger, has more colorful feathers, and has pointed spurs on its legs (difficult to see in photo). The rooster has more prominent and pointy feathers: hackle feathers (neck), cape (feathers down back of neck), saddle feathers (these spill over its sides in front of the tail, like a waterfall), and sickle feathers (long, curving feathers over the tail). The rooster's feathers are also shinier, and the rooster has a larger comb/wattle.

■ Feathers (slide 6): Ask kids to look at the feathers on these birds. What differences do they notice? The feathers have different colors, some have spots, while others have lines, and some feathers are solid in color. Some feathers are fluffy (make particular note of the silkie hen with chicks), some lie flat on the body, and others are raised away from the body (frizzle). Point out the crest on the silkie, and the rooster's tail feathers and feathered legs and feet.

■ What do you know about eggs? (slide 7): Show a picture or a carton of different eggs. Elicit responses about their size, color, and shape. Kids should conclude that eggs come in different shapes and sizes. Ask them questions about the parts of an egg.

■ Parts of an egg (slide 8): Display egg anatomy image and show the parts of an egg: albumen (al-BYOO-men) or white (provides some food for the developing chick), germinal disc or blastoderm (where fertilization happens and from where the chick develops), chalazae or twisters (ropy-like structures that keep the yolk centered in the middle of the albumen), membranes (not labeled; thin, papery layers that line the shell to keep the albumen and yolk safe from bacteria and from drying out), the yolk (the yellow mass that provides food for the developing chick), air cell (bubble), and the shell (the protective layer of calcium that protects the egg, and also has tiny holes to allow air and moisture in and out).

- A chick can grow in an egg (slide 9): Explain that if there is a rooster (daddy chicken) with a hen that lays an egg, the egg can develop into a baby chick. The hen has to sit on the egg to keep it warm for 21 days.
- The eggs hatch! (slide 10): Point out the egg tooth, which the chick uses to break out of the shell. The egg tooth falls off a few days after hatching. Hens can hatch eggs, or humans can hatch them in a special box called an incubator that keeps the air around the eggs moist and warm. The eggs must be turned several times each day. Chicks hatch after 21 days. They are wet when they first hatch. When they dry off, they are covered with fluffy, warm feathers called down.
- Eggs can be good food, too! (slide 11): Explain that not all eggs can become baby chicks. If there is no rooster or if the hen does not sit on the egg, a chick will not develop. We can eat these eggs.
- Let's learn more about chickens (slide 12): Explain to participants that they will go to the different stations to learn more about chickens.
- Next, divide kids into 3 or 4 equal groups of 4 or 5 kids per group. Direct each group to a station, where an adult will guide them through the activity.

Station 1 (Crazy Chickens)

Follow the instructions on the Crazy Chickens lesson. Use the visuals and ask kids to recall some of the parts of a chicken. Review the names of the parts. Describe what each part does. Ask them to identify parts as you point to them.

- *Comb:* Red, fleshy part on the head, releases heat from the body
- *Wattles:* Red, fleshy parts that hang under the beak, release heat from the body

- *Wings:* Used for flight, but most chickens cannot fly very well
- *Beak:* Used for eating, defense, digging in soil, and preening (cleaning and straightening feathers)
- *Tail:* Roosters have long, curved (sickle) tail feathers; hens have shorter, straight tail feathers
- *Feet/Claws:* Used for digging in the soil for food and holding onto perches; also used for self-defense

Have older kids label the parts of the chicken. Everyone can color the drawings.

Facts
- Chickens do not have teeth. They swallow tiny stones, which go into a special organ in the body called a *gizzard.* The stones grind up their food.
- Hens have smaller combs and wattles than roosters.
- Roosters are often more brightly colored than hens.

Station 2 (Fantastic Feathers)

Follow the instructions on the Fantastic Feathers lesson: Ask the children what they know about feathers. Name the different parts of a feather. Show them the parts on the diagram. Show them the feather samples. Point out the different parts and allow them to touch the feathers to feel the differences in each part. Discuss the kinds of feathers. Ask the children what purposes feathers might have. Review the purposes of feathers. Ask what purpose each feather might have. Have kids label and color a feather.

Parts of a Feather
- *Quill:* a hollow, smooth part that attaches the feather to the bird's body
- *Shaft:* central part of the feather that runs up the middle
- *Barb:* parts that grow out from the shaft; tiny hooks act like Velcro or tiny zippers that keep the barbs together
- *Afterfeather:* fuzzy bits at the bottom that look like down

Kinds of Feathers
- *Down:* fuzzy feathers without barbs (like those on a chick), trap heat like a down comforter

- *Flight:* long, strong feathers; push down on the air to push the bird up
- *Contour:* these feathers cover the body smoothly

Purposes of Feathers
- *Allow for flight:* to get away from predators (flight feathers)
- *Warmth:* trap and hold heat in the body (down)
- *Waterproofing:* help rain run off the bird's body (contour)
- *Make the body smooth:* help reduce resistance in flight (contour)

Facts
- Feathers are not naturally waterproof. A chicken rubs its beak on an oil gland at the base of the tail. The oil sticks to the beak. As the bird preens, or arranges its feathers with its beak, it transfers oil to them. The oil helps water run off the feathers.
- Silkie chickens lack barbs on their feathers, which is why their feathers look like animal fur.
- Feathers have a blood supply in the shaft when they are growing. Once the feather is fully grown, the blood supply goes away.

Station 3 (Incredible Eggs)

Follow the instructions on the Incredible Eggs lesson: Ask children to observe the egg and tell what they see. Tell them the names of the parts of an egg. Describe what each part does. Ask them to identify the parts as you point to them. Have them draw an egg. Older kids may want to label the parts on their drawings.

Parts of an Egg
- *Air cell:* provides chick with air when it is almost ready to hatch
- *Albumen* (*al-BYOO-men*): the "white," food for the growing chick
- *Yolk:* main source of food for the growing chick
- *Germinal disc or blastoderm:* place on the yolk where fertilization happens and the chick develops
- *Chalaza* (*chuh-LAH-suh,* singular), *chalazae* (*chuh-LAH-sigh,* plural): "twisters"; look like twisted ropes; keep the yolk centered in the shell as the chick develops

- *Shell:* protects the egg; the shell has tiny holes that allow the chick inside to breathe
- *Shell membranes:* (not shown—between shell and albumen), thin, papery layers that help the growing chick get oxygen, keep egg from drying out, protect from bacteria

Facts
- We can eat fertilized eggs, but eggs from the store are not fertilized.
- There is no difference in nutrition between a brown egg and a white egg. The hen's diet affects the nutritional contents of the egg.

Station 4 (Meet a Chicken): Optional

Sit on a chair with the chicken in your lap. Have paper towels at the ready for any accidents. Have a volunteer get the kids into a line and show them how to use two touching fingers (index and middle fingers side by side, with thumb holding the rest against palm). Allow the kids to touch the chicken one at a time. Be careful not to crowd or overheat the bird. Emphasize gentle, slow movements and instruct them to pet from head to tail, as they would a cat or dog. As they touch, ask: What does she feel like? Is she soft? What color are her eyes? Where do you see scales on her body? Instruct kids to touch the comb, wattle, beak, leg, earlobe, and so on. If the bird is tolerant, you may stretch out a wing or leg, or perhaps pull back the tuft of feathers to expose the ear. As they finish, offer kids hand sanitizer.

RECOMMENDED NEXT PROJECTS

Kids might want to explore an embryology project, using an incubator to hatch chicks. Prior to starting a project of this nature, however, the instructor should find a home for all chicks that hatch, keeping in mind that about 50 percent of them will be male. Another project might involve comparing birds and dinosaurs.

Urban Homesteading
Discover and Activate Your Inner Urban Homesteader

ZACK McCANNON

n this program, adults will be facilitated through three steps in which they identify what "urban homesteading" means to them, are given a modern description of urban homesteading, and learn how to discover and activate their own "inner urban homesteader."

When participants leave the project with an Inner Urban Homesteader Certificate, they are empowered to implement the steps necessary to create an urban homestead of their own. They've now identified and written down what it is that inspires them about homesteading, and they know their favorite common homesteading practices (cooking and food preservation, gardening, crafting, backyard hens, carpentry, beekeeping, composting, seed saving, greenhouse plants, and bartering and commerce).

Age Range	Library Types	Cost Estimate
Adults	Public and academic libraries	$0-$50

FIGURE 24.1 | Urban homesteading at the Bell Urban Farm on Tyler Street in Conway, Arkansas

OVERVIEW

This is a 3-step guide for adults to discover and activate their inner urban homesteader. The program can range between 1 and 2 hours in length. One or 2 staff members facilitating the workshop will suffice. It's recommended to cap the class size at 50 participants. The class instruction is broken down into 3 steps, with continual participation throughout the entire program. Participants should be able to write down their thoughts and ask questions throughout.

NECESSARY EQUIPMENT AND MATERIALS

- Pencil or pen
- Blank piece of paper or notebook
- 1-page printout containing a description of urban homesteading and common homesteading practices
- 1-page printout of an Inner Urban Homesteader Certificate for each participant

STEP-BY-STEP INSTRUCTIONS

Preparation

Provide participants with your own description of urban homesteading and common homesteading practices. Suggested content might include:

- Urban homesteading description: The early use of the word *homesteading* in North America came from the U.S. government granting homesteads to settlers in the nineteenth century. In this context, a few ways of defining homesteading would be, "Life as a settler on a homestead" or "homesteading the land." Urban homesteaders in the twenty-first century may identify more with the practices of early homesteaders than with the economic need to homestead. After all, we have many conveniences today that we didn't have in the nineteenth century. What those early homesteaders did was adopt techniques for maximum sustenance with minimal input. These systems and practices emerged from life-or-death conditions. The simple but effective tools and processes used by the early homesteaders are now the point of difference between a highly mechanized farm and a more humanized homestead. Modern homesteaders seek a lifestyle that reduces the need for big-box and grocery store visits—a self-sufficient way of life that is similar to the simpler lifestyle of the early homesteaders. Urban homesteading leverages a large network of small-scale homesteaders who help each other independently meet the needs of their households.
- Common homesteading practices include:
  - Cooking and food preservation
  - Gardening
  - Crafting
  - Backyard hens
  - Carpentry
  - Beekeeping
  - Composting
  - Seed saving
  - Greenhouse plants
  - Bartering and commerce

Have a pencil and a notebook or blank piece of paper accessible for each participant at the beginning of step 1.

Have the one-page printouts of the urban homesteading description and common homesteading practices available at the beginning of step 2.

Have the printed Inner Urban Homesteader Certificates ready at the beginning of step 3 for participants to sign and to circle their key interest, and then take back to their homestead.

Program Instructions

Step 1

- Have each participant write their name and ask them to write 1–2 paragraphs describing what urban homesteading means to them and what land and home resources they currently have that can be used for homesteading.
- When everyone has finished writing, ask participants to circle 3 words that inspire them from their personal description of urban homesteading. (You will direct them back to those three words later in step 3.)

Step 2

- Hand each participant a copy of the 1-page urban homesteading description and common homesteading practices printout that you created in preparation for this program.
- Read this document to the group and use this opportunity to highlight your knowledge of urban homesteading. Open a discussion on how urban homesteading differs from the traditional (historical) definition of homesteading.
- Ask participants to circle 3 words from the urban homesteading description and 3 words from the common homesteading practices that might inspire them to establish their own urban homestead. (You will direct them back to these 6 words later in step 3.)

Step 3

- Hand each participant an Inner Urban Homesteader Certificate.
- Direct participants to write the 3 words that inspired them from step 1 and 6 of the words that inspired them from step 2 on their certificate in the space provided.
- Ask if anyone would like to share their words and help facilitate like-minded homesteaders by allowing time for contact exchanges.
- Finally, congratulate participants on discovering and activating their inner urban homesteader and have them sign their certificate.
- Optional bonus instruction will be to have participants come up with a name for their urban homestead by printing it after their signed name.
- Make sure participants take all their documents with them to reference at their urban homestead.

RECOMMENDED NEXT PROJECTS

After participants have discovered and activated their inner urban homesteader, they will be eager for more instruction on the finer details of homesteading. You might consider offering future gardening programs that close the food loop, like planting from seed in the ground, keeping a greenhouse, or harvesting open-pollinated seeds for the next growing season. Raising your own chickens closes food loops in many different ways, and it provides a fresh and healthy protein source every day in the form of their eggs. "Closing the food loop" means that participants are actively involved in natural ecological systems that produce food or help facilitate the production of food and culture through craft, which will shape their day-to-day decisions and create a natural transition into urban homesteading.

How to Start a Hobby Farm

ELLYSSA KROSKI

magine having your own herd of miniature pygmy goats that excitedly gallop across the yard to greet you every day, or a flock of chickens that will follow along in step as you walk, chirping all the while, or a sheep that will baa "hello" to you each time you pass by. Imagine also carrying a basket filled to the brim with vegetables, fruits, herbs, and flowers that you've harvested from your own gardens. This is what it's like to live on a hobby farm.

A hobby farm is a small farm or homestead in which livestock animals such as goats, sheep, pigs, and chickens are raised and crops are grown purely for the enjoyment or sustenance of the owner rather than as a primary source of income. Although hobby farmers may make supplemental income from selling farm by-products such as eggs, milk, offspring, and so on, the owner does not depend on that money in order to live. These dream farms can provide owners with a sustainable source of food between garden crops, eggs and meat from poultry, and milk and meat from livestock—not to mention the tranquility of farm life and the delight of raising farm animals.

Libraries have moved steadily toward providing patrons with sustainable living instruction, particularly in recent years amid turbulent times. As this inclination grows, libraries can continue to offer valuable programming in this area by guiding patrons on their journey to create their own hobby farm.

Age Range	Library Types	Cost Estimate
Adults	Public and academic libraries	$0

OVERVIEW

This program could consist of a single session discussing how to start a hobby farm, or it could be the first in a series of workshops, with guest speakers offering deep dives on subjects such as local laws and purchasing land, building animal shelters, gardening, and assorted livestock topics such as raising sheep, owning goats, setting up a chicken brooder, and so on. This program provides details on how to start to create a hobby farm, which librarians can pass along to patrons during the initial session.

NECESSARY EQUIPMENT AND MATERIALS

- PowerPoint presentation and/or prepared discussion

Recommended but Optional Materials

- Guest speakers from local farms
- S. Weaver, A.L. Hansen, C. Langlois, A.B. McFarlen, and C. McLaughlin, *Hobby Farm Animals* (2015).

STEP-BY-STEP INSTRUCTIONS

Preparation

Librarians can prepare for this session by putting together a discussion (based on the program instructions), a slideshow presentation, or a Q&A session.

FIGURE 25.1 | A young lamb enjoys the warm breeze on a hobby farm.

FIGURE 25.2 | Both goats and chickens love pumpkins, which are a natural de-wormer and are highly nutritious.

Program Instructions

Start Small but Dream Big

Librarians can instruct patrons to think about what they'd like to create and what their dream hobby farm would look like. Patrons may begin by drawing out a plan or simply listing the areas they would like to develop, such as the types of livestock they want to raise and the location of gardens, barns, pathways, chicken coops, and so on. Common hobby farm animals include goats, sheep, cows, horses, donkeys, miniature horses, rabbits, turkeys, chickens, ducks, geese, guinea fowl, and more. The best way to dip a toe in the water is to choose one animal type to begin with and go from there. Chickens are an easy starter animal because they are quite low-maintenance. They are also smart, friendly, and entertaining, and the females provide a dependable food source almost daily (most chickens lay an egg about every 26 hours).

Stay in Your Zone

Librarians can direct patrons to be sure to check any local laws that govern what types of animals they're allowed to own on their property. They can start with the county's zoning office. Officials there will be able to inform patrons if their property is zoned as residential or agricultural and what restrictions may be in place. Some properties may have certain limitations if they are within city limits (versus outside the city) or simply because of quirky neighborhood guidelines. For example, my property is zoned as agricultural, meaning that nearly any livestock animal can be owned, but all the properties on my street were once part of a neighborhood which passed a set of guidelines more than twenty-five years ago prohibiting "the raising of live swine." Those old restrictions are still technically in place, even though there is no longer anything indicating that a community once existed here. Consequently, none of us can own pigs unless we want to risk a fine. On the other side of the coin, some locales, even if zoned as strictly residential, have recently passed laws that allow for the ownership of chickens. And to make things even more complicated, some areas allow chickens but not roosters due to the noise that they make (it's a myth that they only crow in the morning). So, some due diligence at the outset will avoid pitfalls down the line.

Gimme Shelter

Novice hobby farmers will want to have an appropriate shelter built and in place before they purchase any livestock. Even if they are only starting by adopting baby chicks, these grow up incredibly fast and go from brooder box to chicken coop in no time. There are an inordinate number of books, YouTube videos, and online written step-by-step tutorials detailing how to build shelters of all types for animals, many of which involve upcycling freely available and often discarded materials such as wooden pallets. Small shelters such as chicken coops and rabbit hutches can also be purchased at local feed and grain stores as well as on Amazon. An alternative would be to hire a contractor to build one to specifications.

One other consideration to keep in mind is whether a fence is necessary to keep animals within a pasture for daytime grazing. If that's the case, patrons will want to be sure to research the type of fencing appropriate for each animal type that will share the pasture. A fence for horses will be inadequate for keeping goats, which will easily and almost certainly escape, if only to see if they can.

What's for Dinner?

Many hobby farm animals can subsist on a diet of simple pasture grass and hay, along with salt and some mineral supplements. Sheep and goats, for example, are both ruminants that will happily browse for tasty grass and weeds in the summer and munch on hay all winter and be delighted. But preliminary research is recommended for whatever type of animal patrons will want to raise, whether through books, videos, or by talking to people in the many Facebook groups on that animal type. Careful study will prevent beginner mistakes such as purchasing goat feed pellets and offering them free choice to animals that can and probably will gorge themselves on it, resulting in a serious condition called bloat.

What's Up, Doc?

Before purchasing any animals, it is important to investigate whether there is a veterinarian that services livestock or "large animals" in the area. Some of these types of vets offer a mobile service in which they will come out to the farm and make "house calls" on livestock animals. It's definitely recommended that animals are looked at shortly after purchase to make sure that they aren't carrying any diseases or parasites, get their shots, and get a de-worming treatment. This is especially important if other animals are already in place and will share the same pasture. A separate quarantine area may be developed for adding new animals to the herd that will keep the others safe until the new adoptions can be seen by the vet; this space will also allow owners to slowly introduce the newcomers to the existing crowd.

This same vet may also offer a hoof-trimming service for animals such as sheep and goats that will need such maintenance on an ongoing basis. This is very helpful, as rookie hobby farmers can ask the vet to demonstrate how they can do this themselves with a pair of hoof trimmers.

Purchasing Animals

Once all this research and preparation is complete, there are many ways to go about purchasing animals, such as through local Craigslist listings, organized "flock swaps," livestock auctions, and by reaching out to the community to get recommendations for reputable breeders in the area through town or county Facebook groups, and so on.

Keeping animals is a rewarding experience, and even more so if the animal that is chosen is the right fit for one's goals and abilities. It is important to know that there are many different breeds for each animal type, with each breed possessing a different temperament, weight range, size, and maintenance requirements, so some additional research may be required to find just the right match. For example, some goat breeds such as the Boer can get quite large, weighing in at over 200 pounds on average, while miniature Pygmy goats may barely top 25 pounds. Novice farmers may find a smaller goat breed such as the Pygmy or the Nigerian Dwarf easier to handle than a heftier one. Moreover, different breeds can bring with them different characteristics, such as the Tennessee fainting goat, which may pass out and fall over if nervous. And in addition to having distinct characteristics, animal breeds can have noticeable differences in levels of maintenance or upkeep. For example, novice farmers may be reluctant to adopt sheep, which must be shorn each spring, but there are a handful of "hair sheep" breeds such as the Katahdin, named after the tallest peak in Maine, which need no such attention annually.

Gender should be another consideration. The males of some livestock animals such as goats can be quite aggressive, which may be challenging for new owners, but a castrated male goat, called a wether, can be just as docile as the females of the breed.

The age of the animal is another factor to bear in mind. Adoption at a young age will increase the bond formed between the owner and the animal, but caution should be exercised when purchasing "bottle babies" as an induction into livestock ownership. Bottle babies are animals that have been taken from their mothers before they have finished the weaning process, and they will need much care and attention, including feeding them from a bottle every few hours. This may be overly stressful for new owners, in addition to being extremely time-consuming.

Growing Your Own

There are so many exciting ways to garden available, and there really is something for everyone in this practice. There is so much to choose from between raised gardens, container gardening, vertical gardening, straw bale gardening (see chapter 5), and plain-old, tilled gardens in the ground. My inclination is toward container and raised gardening, as I live in an area overpopulated with fire ants. Additionally, I prefer to control what type of soil I garden with, and raised beds such as my Vegepods—(https://vegepod.com), waist-high, self-watering beds that come with a canopy to protect from harsh UV rays and garden pests, as well as an optional hothouse cover for starting a garden early in the season—and straw bale gardens allow me to do just that.

In addition to the different methods available, gardeners may choose to divide their efforts into multiple smaller gardens according to different themes such as:

- A simple *herb garden* complete with all the herbs and spices gardeners prefer to cook with, such as rosemary, thyme, dill, basil, parsley, and oregano.
- A *pizza garden* that yields basil, oregano, parsley, onions, garlic, tomatoes, and bell peppers.

FIGURE 25.3 | Enclosed vegepods make the perfect raised containers for an herb garden.

- A *nacho garden* with cilantro, onions, tomatoes, and jalapeno peppers.
- A *tea garden* with chamomile, mint, pineapple sage, and lemon verbena.
- A *medicinal garden* that yields echinacea, mint, lavender, feverfew, and sage.
- An *herbs de Provence* garden with thyme, rosemary, fennel, savory, marjoram, tarragon, basil, chervil, mint, oregano, and lavender.
- A *moon garden* with flowers that only bloom at night, as well as those which are most visible after dark such as white or silver flowers. These may include the moonflower, creeping phlox, hydrangea, evening primrose, angel's trumpet, and more.[1]

Succession Planting

One effective method that hobby farmers and gardeners use is to stagger the planting of crops in order to spread out the harvest over weeks or months. For example, if growing crops from seed, one may plant enough seeds for 4 to 6 tomato or cucumber plants early in the season and follow that up with 4 to 6 more a month later, so that the plants will mature and produce vegetables at a staggered rate, extending the harvest season.

A Little Neighborly Advice

Whatever method of gardening is chosen, one of the best sources for advice will always be those who live in the area. Neighbors and locals can offer a unique perspective as to what amendments work best in an area's soil, what time of year the last frost is likely to occur, what plants grow best in a particular area, and what plants just will not grow in that particular climate. So, it's always a good idea to check in with the locals before getting started.

RECOMMENDED NEXT PROJECTS

This program was a broad overview of what a hobby farm is and things to consider when contemplating starting one. Going forward, librarians can develop more focused programs and instructional workshops covering single topics such as raising goats, container gardening, or breeding animals, and they may invite guest speakers to join them. The library may also start a hobby farmers club or a library garden club.

NOTE

1. M. Shaffer, *Planning & Planting a Moon Garden* (North Adams, MA: Storey Publishing, 2001).

ABOUT THE
CONTRIBUTORS

MAGGIE PINNICK ANDREJKO graduated with an MLS degree from Indiana University-Purdue University Indianapolis in 2019. She is now the adult/ teen program coordinator at the Mulvane Public Library in Kansas. She enjoys spending time with her husband and dog, exploring new parks, and attempting (and sometimes succeeding at) new crafts.

LAUREN ANTOLINO is the head of children's services at the Cranford (NJ) Public Library.

DANA BRIGANDI is the director of development, marketing, and programming at the James V. Brown Library in Williamsport, Pennsylvania. She has designed and created programs for adults of all abilities, and she hosted, with her youngest daughter, a variety of do-it-yourself videos on the Brown Library's YouTube channel.

ELLEN LUMPKIN BROWN is a designer, instructor, author, and entrepreneur who introduces library patrons to the wonders of sewing both virtually and in-person. *School Library Journal* spotlighted her work in a national review of innovative library programs. She was the featured speaker at the New Jersey Maker's Day Makerspace Professional Development Training for librarians.

MARTHA NAPOLITAN COWNAP is the herb gardener at Camphill Village Kimberton Hills, a farming community in Chester County, Pennsylvania, that includes adults with special needs (www.camphillkimberton.org). She has been making friends with plants for over fifty years. She enjoys leading herb workshops and wild plant walks in southeastern Pennsylvania.

COLLEEN ELLITHORPE is currently digital services librarian at the Voorheesville (NY) Public Library. She graduated from SUNY Albany's MSIS program in 2014 and has since created hundreds of unique programs for patrons of all ages. Colleen is a former blogger for the ALA's Programming Librarian website and is a graduate of the Sunshine State Library Leadership Institute.

ANNA FRANTZ has been a librarian with the Public Library Albuquerque & Bernalillo County system in Albuquerque, New Mexico, for almost three years. She plans programs for adults, often coordinating with outside experts to speak on a variety of different subjects. She has her MLS degree from Emporia State University.

JENNIFER GARGIULO is the manager of Ives Squared, a makerspace and entrepreneurial hub for the greater New Haven, Connecticut, community that is supported by CT Next and the New Haven Innovation Collaborative. She previously worked in the children's department of the New Haven Free Public Library as a STEAM librarian. Jennifer is passionate about intergenerational programming.

GABRIELLE GRIFFIS is the assistant youth services librarian at the Brewster Ladies' Library in Brewster, Massachusetts. She is a member of the Blue Marble Librarians, as well as a repair event organizer and enthusiast. She is a contributing author to the books *Libraries and Sustainability: Programs and Practices for Community Impact* and *Repair Revolution: How Fixers Are Transforming Our Throwaway Culture* and is available for speaking events. You can connect with her at gabriellegriffis.com or on Twitter @ggriffiss.

NANCY GRIFFITHS is a paraprofessional librarian with an MFA in dramaturgy. She facilitated a seed library collection for over three years, and she continues to create garden and nature-related displays and to teach and coordinate nature connection and garden-related programs. Nancy has been a gardener for over twenty years.

ANGELA HOGG is a certified elementary teacher mother of three. Angela and her husband began hatching and raising chicks three years ago with their kids and enjoy teaching others how to do the same.

VELYA JANCZ-URBAN is a teacher, author, former Brazilian dairy farm owner, proponent of medical freedom, and "herstory unsanitized" expert. Her daughter **EHRIS URBAN** is a green witch, herbalist, holistic nutritionist, author, Reiki master, flower essence therapy practitioner, and a graduate of the New England School of Homeopathy. This funny and frank mother/daughter duo connect with audiences through their green witch workshops, herstory unsanitized presentations, books, and herb school. Learn more at groundedgoodwife.com.

CATHERINE JOHNSON is passionate about the environment and the power of neighboring. She works to inspire eco-mindedness by having fun stewarding natural resources. She is also a cofounder of the Neighboring Movement nonprofit and works to connect neighbors in her neighborhood in Wichita, Kansas.

MARISSA LIEBERMAN is the head of reference services at the Cranford (NJ) Public Library.

ZACK McCANNON is a co-owner of Bell Urban Farm in Conway, Arkansas, with his wife Kim and two boys. The Bell Urban Farm has chickens, bees, flowers, vegetables, herbs, a seed garden, workshops, their home, and a local-foods grocery store called the Farmstand. Zack was the garden programmer at the Faulkner County Library in 2020–21. He can be found at https://bellurbanfarm.com.

KATE McCARTY has been the food systems professional at the University of Maine Cooperative Extension since 2009. She has completed the Master Food Preserver program, an intensive, hands-on training in all aspects of home food preservation. Kate manages the volunteer efforts of the sixty-plus Master Food Preserver volunteers statewide and teaches food preservation programs in six Maine counties.

ALLISON CICERO MOORE is an artist and educator. She opened Shandon Street Soapery (in Columbia, SC) in 2020, sharing her passion for craftsmanship and design through naturally scented luxury soaps. You can often find Moore selling soaps at markets, packing online orders, or teaching workshops at the Columbia Museum of Art, the Richland Library, and other institutions.

JENNIFER MURTOFF, of Home to Roost LLC (https://htrchickens.com), is a farmer's granddaughter who provides compassionate consulting care for backyard chickens in the Chicagoland area and beyond. A professional editor, she also works on chicken-related materials and teaches programs for schools, libraries, and community organizations, both in-person and virtually. You can connect with her at 708-259-6877 or at hometoroostllc@gmail.com.

VERONIQUE PAILLARD-BAUMANN is a desk assistant and designer of adult crafts at the Cranford (NJ) Public Library.

ELIZABETH PEIRCE is a writer, editor, and educator living on the east coast of Canada. She has written several books on gardening and preserving topics, including *Grow Hope: A Simple Guide to Creating Your Own Food Garden at Home,* and *You Can Too! Canning, Pickling and Preserving the Maritime Harvest.* You can visit her website at elizabethpeirce.ca.

MARIA PORTELOS-ROMETO is a family and consumer sciences agent for the University of Florida/IFAS Extension and has been an educator for forty years. Her academic training includes a doctorate and master's degree in educational leadership, and a BS degree in food science. She holds certification as a Food Preservationist from Cornell University and is ServSafe certified.

LYNNE SERPE is a certified Master Composter and an avid reader. She ran thousands of food waste collection programs with the Queens Library and New Orleans Public Library systems. She founded and runs Compost NOW (New Orleans Waste) at www.compost-now.org and is also the sustainability coordinator for the New Orleans Jazz and Heritage Festival.

ROSE SIMPSON is a community technology librarian at the New Haven (CT) Free Public Library, where she manages the library's makerspace, the Tinker Lab. She has spent many years running science, technology, and maker programs in the children, teen, and adult departments of several libraries in Connecticut.

CELESTE TAPIA is a library technical assistant in Ives Squared at the New Haven (CT) Free Public Library. She has spearheaded many successful creative and entrepreneurial programs at the library. A native Argentinian, she is currently pursuing her MLS degree.

KRISTIN WHITE has over ten years of experience with homesteading. She loves homesteading so much that she started her own business teaching others how to homestead. Prior to starting her business, Chicken Librarian, she worked as a librarian in public and academic libraries. You can find more about her at chickenlibrarian.com.

DEREK WOLFGRAM is the director of the Redwood City Public Library in California, where he focuses on community collaborations, equity and inclusion efforts, and creating experiences to help people share the joys of literacy and learning. His twenty-five-year career in public libraries has included management and administrative roles with three other libraries.

INDEX

roosters, 148, 150, 157–159, 172.
  See also chickens
rosemary, 66–67, 175–176

S
safety discussions, 117
Sashiko stitching, 99, 103
sauerkraut, 45–49
scented oils, for soapmaking,
  106, 107, 109, 114
seeds, growing, 9–15, 24–26,
  27–33
senior programs, 81–85, 87–91.
  See also adult programs
Serpe, Lynne, 131–136, 182
Sew It! By Hand (Brown), 103
Sew It! Workshop videos, 103
sewing by hand, 93–103
sheep, xvii, 169–175
simple syrups, 51–54
Simpson, Rose, 17–22, 182
skullcap, 64, 67, 68
soapmaking, 105–110,
  111–121
sock heating pads, 64–67
spearmint, 61, 66–67
spores, 19–21
stevia, 61
stitching, 93–103
straw bale gardening, xvi, 27–33
Straw Bale Gardens Complete
  (Karsten), xvi, 28, 29
succession planting, 176–177
sulfur dips, 57
sustainability experts,
  oordinating with, 3–7
syrup-making, 51–54

T
Tapia, Celeste, 23–26, 81–85, 182
teas, herbal, 59–62
teen programs. *See* young adult
  programs
thermometers, 113, 118, 138, 140
thread patches, 98*f*, 100–102*f*
Tractor Supply, 146, 149
tulsi tea, 61
tween programs
  on gardening, 3–7, 17–22, 27–33
  on homesteading, 125–129, 131–136,
    153–161
  on pioneer crafts, 71–75, 81–85,
    93–103, 105–110
  on preservation, 45–49, 55–58, 59–62

U
University of Maine Cooperative
  Extension, 37, 39, 41, 43–44
UpCycle That! website, 91
upcycled jewelry, 87–91
Urban, Ehris, 63–68, 180
urban exodus, xiii
urban homesteading, 163–167
USDA, 30, 39, 40–41

V
vegepods, 175, 176*f*
vegetables
  dehydrating, 55–58
  fermenting, 45–49
  growing, 9–15, 27–33
  pickling, 37–44
vermicomposting, 6, 136, 142
veterinarians, 173–174
vinegar, 39, 40, 41, 42, 120

W

wallpaper gift bags, 77–80

waste collection programs, 131–136

watering plants, 14–15

White, Kristin, 51–54, 182

Wild Fermentation (Katz), 48

windy whisp stitches, 98*f*, 102

winter, growing vegetables in, 9–15

Wolfgram, Derek, 125–129, 182

worms

    as chicken food, 145, 151, 156

    composting with, 6, 136, 142

woven thread patches, 98*f*, 100–102*f*

Y

yolks, 158, 160

young adult programs

    on gardening, 3–7, 17–22, 23–26, 27–33

    on homesteading, 125–129, 131–136

    on pioneer crafts, 71–75, 81–85, 87–91, 93–103, 105–110, 111–121

    on preservation, 37–44, 45–49, 55–58, 59–62, 63–68

YouTube videos, 91, 120, 173

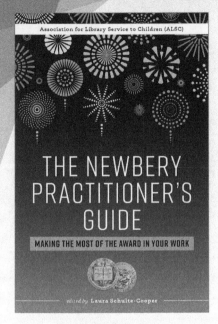

Printed in the USA
CPSIA information can be obtained
at www.ICGtesting.com
JSHW012010240124
55787JS00003B/6